For Miloš Jiránek

Bringing up babies and young children who have very special needs

A 21st century guide for parents, students and new practitioners

**Bringing up babies and young children
who have very special needs**

ISBN 978-0-9576601-6-8

Printed and bound in the UK by 4edge Ltd, Hockley

Illustrations © Martina Jirankova-Limbrick 2019

About the author

Peter Limbrick had a brother with cerebral palsy born just before he went to study zoology at Liverpool University. Nicholas died at forty years of age.

Peter's career has taken him into special schools as both teacher and senior manager and into two voluntary projects as director: One-to-One and One Hundred Hours. One-to-One was part of the UK movement in the 1970s to get children and adults with intellectual disabilities out of institutional care. One Hundred Hours in the 1990s pioneered keyworker support for families whose baby had neurological impairment.

From his One Hundred Hours experience, Peter developed and published the Team Around the Child (TAC) approach in 2001 and has promoted this in Australia, Canada, Croatia, Czech Republic, Ireland, Sweden and the UK.

Peter lives in the Black Mountains on the border between England and Wales where he edits the international Interconnections News Service and its online TAC Bulletin about babies, children and young adults who are disabled, marginalised or vulnerable.

Contact:
Interconnections
E-mail: peter.limbrick@teamaroundthechild.com
Web: http://tacinterconnections.com

Books by Peter Limbrick published by Interconnections

The Team Around the Child: Multi-agency service co-ordination for children with complex needs and their families. (2001)

An Integrated Pathway for Assessment and Support: For children with complex needs and their families. (2003)

Early Support for Children with Complex Needs: Team Around the Child and the Multi-agency Keyworker. (2004)

TAC for the 21st Century: Nine essays on Team Around the Child. (2009)

Horizontal Teamwork in a Vertical World: Exploring interagency collaboration and people empowerment. (2012)

Caring Activism: A 21st century concept of care. (2016)

Early Childhood Intervention without Tears: Improved support for infants with disabilities and their families. (2017)

Primary Interventionists in the Team Around the Child Approach (TAC): A guide for managers and practitioners supporting families whose baby or infant has a multifaceted condition (2018)

Edited by Peter Limbrick:

One-to-One: An experiment in community participation in long-stay hospitals. (1976) Published by Inter-Action Trust

Family-Centred Support for Children with Disabilities and Special Needs: A collection of essays. (2007) Published by Interconnections

Interconnections Bookshop:

http://www.tacinterconnections.com/index.php/bookshop

Lost in a labyrinth of country lanes, a driver asked a villager for directions to the airport. The surprised villager replied, "The airport? I wouldn't start from here if I were you!"

Similarly, if I were given the task of designing effective support for babies and young children who have very special needs and their families, I would not start from where we are now in the UK.

(Peter Limbrick)

Contents

Introduction

This small book is written for people who are coming new to the world of babies and young children who have very special needs. I hope this will include new parents, others with a parenting role, family members, students who might eventually work with these children and people who have just moved into this field of work. It can often feel like a world separated from the main world because babies and infants who have very special needs belong to a small minority most people will not encounter very often if at all.

I have used the phrase 'bringing up' in the book's title, because this is what parents all around the world do and it is what this book is about. Parents bring up their children as best they can whatever abilities and needs their children have. But, unfortunately, when a baby or young child has very special needs it can feel that some of this parenting role is taken over by one or more practitioners[1]. Parents might then find themselves inappropriately forced into a secondary or subservient role because practitioners appear as experts and because parents do not yet know all the same things the practitioners know.

---

[1] I am using the term 'practitioner' to refer to all people who work in some capacity with these babies and young children and their families. This includes people providing health, education or family support in public, private or voluntary agencies.

This book, then, is about parents bringing up their young children and how the main task of agencies and their practitioners in both hospital and community-based services is to respect and support parents in this role. There is very clear recognition here that parents have the most important role and responsibility. The treatments and programmes provided by practitioners must be supplementary to and supportive of this parental role. While an ideal is some sort of partnership, parents must be in the leading role making the important decisions about support for their child and family.

It is common in every country for parents of all young children to ask for help when they need it – during pregnancy, after the birth or in the coming months and years. The up-to-date support I am describing in this book follows this natural approach. In this, parents bring up their babies and infants who have very special needs as best they can and ask for help when they need it. Roles are very clear in this:

- Babies and young children belongs to their parents.
- Parents carry the right and responsibility to bring up their children.
- Agencies and their practitioners carry the professional responsibility to offer relevant and effective support when invited to do so.

In my experience, most parents of babies and infants who have very special needs will want support and will appreciate relevant help that comes when it is needed. If parents are fortunate, practitioners will listen very carefully to them about what is needed before they begin helping.

The babies and young children I am writing about

'Very special needs' is not a scientific term or one that is a recognised in hospitals, clinics or schools. But it fits this book because it suggest a spectrum at one end of which are children whose special needs are largely straightforward and, at the other end, children who have a collection of diagnoses and conditions that are complex and often hard to fathom. This book is about the latter. Included in 'very special needs' are conditions and impairments that influence how well a child sees, hears, thinks, moves, uses hands, communicates, learns, behaves and relates to other children and adults. This list embraces children who have a diagnosis of autism.

Babies and young children who have very special needs might have a genetic syndrome. They might also have medical conditions that require, for instance, nasogastric tubes, an oxygen supply and a regime of essential medications in hospital or at home. Some will have a short or uncertain life expectancy.

When planning support to help these infants learn, rather than describing them as having multiple or complex disabilities, I prefer to say they each have their own single unique multifaceted condition. When we stop thinking in multiples, we can find less complicated and more effective ways to support each child's development and learning. Readers will quickly see if I am writing about children they are concerned for. Much of what I say in this book, though, will be relevant to parents, students and practitioners of children at all parts of the spectrum of special needs.

In this book I will focus more on babies and young children's learning than on their health issues. This comes naturally to me as a teacher, but I acknowledge that health, development and learning influence each other. Part of my appeal in this book is for babies and young children to have earlier help with their learning or education. I will also give some focus to family support drawing on my experience as a family keyworker.

My phrases 'babies and young children' or 'babies and infants' both refers to babies and infants up to school age. These first months and years can be a challenging time for families as they adapt to a new life with a child who has very special needs. After these first busy years, many families find life settles down into calmer times with the new child requiring less special attention and taking their rightful place as a valued member of family, nursery and school.

For some babies and infants who have very special needs, some relevant support has traditionally come in many countries under the name of 'early childhood intervention' (ECI). This type of support has grown since the middle of the last century as a predominantly medical mode using practitioners available in hospitals and clinics. In some localities, teachers are also involved. In my experience, babies and young children who have a multifaceted condition have brought to light some confusions in early childhood intervention about what therapy is and what education is. They are traditionally thought of as separate from each other and offered to children as separate interventions. This fragmented approach loses its validity when helping an infant in such natural activities as managing clothes, using cup or spoon, and moving across a room to fetch a ball. Should therapists or teachers support this learning? I will argue in this book for a degree of integration of the two on the basis that keeping them totally separate makes no sense and brings serious disadvantages to children, families and practitioners.

Perhaps in the future, there will be fully qualified practitioners for early child and family support trained to bring everything together for new children who have a multifaceted condition and their families. Because these children need their practitioners to have very specialist knowledge, I imagine training would have a thorough foundation of whole-child understanding followed by a chosen specialism in movement, communication, play, cognition, etc.

In the absence of such all-round practitioners, the Team Around the Child (TAC) approach[2] has been designed to bring parent and practitioners together to support an individual child and family. The early child and family support I will describe in this book is based on the TAC approach.

The Team Around the Child approach (TAC)

The principles and practice of the Team Around the Child approach or 'TAC' are free for any agency and practitioner to use. The term 'TAC' is used in two ways in this book. In its wider sense, it refers to the TAC

---

[2] Limbrick, P. (2001) *Team Around the Child: Multi-agency service co-ordination for children with complex needs and their families.* UK: Interconnections and
Limbrick, P. (2009) *TAC for the 21st Century: Nine essays on Team Around the Child.* UK: Interconnections

approach. In its narrow sense it refers to an individual child's TAC team. TAC is used in many countries and people can adopt this approach without applying for permission from anyone. The downside of this is that some out-dated agencies describe their work as TAC when it is clearly not. These false TAC projects are likely to disempower parents, treat children in bits and blindly follow a medical mode when it is not appropriate on its own.

In the TAC approach, the two or three main practitioners around a baby or infant agree to meet together regularly with parents to share observations and make a unified plan of action for the child and family. This shared commitment by practitioners and parents to meet face to face as a small, individualised and mutually respectful team defines the TAC approach. The 'main practitioners' are those teachers, therapists, psychologists or others who have the most regular and practical involvement in the child's development and learning. The essence of TAC is genuine teamwork to which each member, whether practitioner or parent, contributes their knowledge, experience, and skills. TAC is characterised by collective caring, concern, commitment and competence. Shared expertise, imagination and creativity lead to a unique and multifaceted plan of action for each unique child and family.

Because it is genuine teamwork, TAC depends on its members being able to relate to each other with honesty, respect and trust. Each TAC can advocate strongly for its child and family because its members know more about them than anyone else does and because each TAC action plan corresponds with parents' wishes. The TAC approach considers the needs of both child and family knowing that helping one helps the other, but also knowing that child and family have very different sets of needs.

A major part of each TAC's function is to promote the baby or infant's learning. In TAC discussions, education and therapy programmes can be integrated into a whole approach to support the child's care, socialising, play and everyday activity (washing, eating and drinking, managing clothes, bath time, bedtime, etc).

An important element that supports all aspects of the TAC approach is the keyworker[3]. This is the TAC practitioner who has most close contact with the child and family. They are the first person parents will usually contact when help is needed with a new challenge and are recognised by the wider group of people supporting the child and family as the person who can link everything together.

Taking a wider view of TAC, the advantages it brings to children, families and practitioners include the following:

- Parents are acknowledged, respected and supported as the people carrying the right and responsibility to bring up their child and are partners in their child's TAC.
- Parents have a keyworker – one special person they get on well with and trust for emotional support and who helps keep all elements of support linked together and well organised.
- From the beginning, a rounded picture is built up of the whole child living and learning within a family setting.
- The child's abilities in moving, seeing, hearing, communicating, cognition, etc are understood to connect with each other and to be supportive of each other as the child learns.
- Babyhood and infancy are respected – preventing the new child being overloaded and stressed with too many programmes and too many non-family adults.
- Family life is protected and nurtured – preventing parents being kept too busy and stressed with too many appointments in too many different locations.
- The collective effort nurtures and protects child-parent attachment.

---

[3] Limbrick-Spencer, G. (2001) *The Keyworker: a practical guide.* Birmingham: WordWorks with Handsel Trust
In this book the keyworker is defined as: *...a source of support for the families of children with disabilities and a conduit by which other services are accessed and used effectively.* (p 7)

- The collective effort safeguards the quality of life of the new child and of the whole family.
- Practitioners belong now to a small mutually supportive team in which they can enhance their knowledge of all aspects of child development and learning.

Each and every baby and infant in the world comes and grows as an integrated whole child involved in natural everyday activities. (Exceptions include those brought up in institutional care and in deprived and abusive situations.) New understanding and skills integrate the various child development components of communication, perception, cognition, movement, etc. We can describe TAC as the effort for the key people around the child to achieve the same integrated wholeness with each other in their work with each of these new children.

Early child and family support

Early child and family support is my preferred term to replace 'early childhood intervention' and 'early support'. This term brings families clearly into the picture. The early child and family support I will describe is offered as an ideal to work towards. How far a child and family's support can move in this direction will depend on the child, parents, practitioners and the situation at the time.

Put briefly, effective early child and family support focuses equally on the baby or young child and the family. These are two different sets of needs but are both equally deserving of support in the first hours, days, weeks, months and pre-school years. In this, parents are respected and supported as the people who carry the responsibility of bringing up their children and practitioners work to support parents in this role. Children are respected and valued and attachment between child and parents is nurtured. At the same time, the quality of life of child and family is a continuing priority. The baby or infant's development and learning programmes come to them as natural baby or infant activity, firstly in their own home and then in any playgroups, nurseries and children's centres they attend.

My suggestions for early child and family support fit for the 21st century come mostly from my direct experience during four decades of working with babies and young children who have a multifaceted condition and their families. All that I say in this book comes from my direct experience unless I am quoting another author. Each of the main elements of the effective support I will describe are already benefitting some children and families in my country and others, but I know of very few examples of all elements being used together. Children, their families and particular practitioners have been my most important teachers. I have learned that all children are unique, all families are unique, all practitioners are unique.

I hope this book shows respect for children, parents and practitioners and avoids all unjustified generalisations. It will enable parents to compare the support they are getting with the early child and family support I describe. Students will see whether their training is out of date or modern. Practitioners coming new to this field of work will see if their employing agency is stuck in inappropriate medical or institutional attitudes.

1

The three pillars of early child and family support

An effective system for early child and family support must have three modes to meet three interconnected sets of needs. These are the medical mode, the education mode and the family-support mode. There are too many varying and over-lapping factors for exact definitions, but there follows an account of how I characterise the three modes and the people involved in them.

The medical mode

The main practitioners in the medical mode will include neonatologists, paediatricians, paediatric nurses, therapists and auxiliaries. These are likely to be the first people helping the child in hospital, surgery, clinic or centre to support the child's survival, freedom from pain, health, development and wellbeing. There will be a need for the child to travel to various places near or far for treatment. There can be repeated waiting lists. Some medical practitioners will do home visits. Many babies who have very special needs spend their first days, weeks or months in hospital in a neonatal intensive care unit (NICU) or a special care baby unit (SCBU) after which they go home and might start getting some relevant support from community-based health agencies while, perhaps, still needing some hospital-based support.

The education mode

The main practitioners here will be teachers, nursery staff, assistants, key-workers and perhaps psychologists in pre-schools, nurseries and children's centres. There can be specialist teachers for children with special needs in, for example, behaviour, communication, hearing or vision. Some education practitioners will do home visits. The education mode focuses on the child's play, development, learning and wellbeing, promoting the emergence of new understanding and skills.

The family support mode

The people involved in family support can include any of the above practitioners, social workers, counsellors, family-support workers and keyworkers. They support parents in their upbringing role and recognise the family will have needs that arise from the very special needs of the child. In the family support mode parents, siblings and grandparents will be taken account of as well as other significant people who are thought of as 'family'.

*

There is much overlap between these three modes. Sometimes, traditional support comes to the child and family as a package with two or three modes wrapped together. For instance, NICUs and SCBUs might have a social worker in attendance to address some family needs. Therapists from health services can support children in nurseries and children's centres. A child development centre (CDC) might have medical, therapy, teaching and social work input.

Such examples of integration are very welcome because they recognise the child and family have a range of different needs and, importantly, that outcomes are improved when the practitioners around each child work closely together. The opposite side of this coin are localities in which a child's practitioners choose to work independently without co-operating with each other. The result then can be fragmentation, confusion and chaos.

Throughout his book with the medical, education and family support modes in mind, I am suggesting effective early child and family support has three essential and equally important pillars: Health, Education and Family Support.

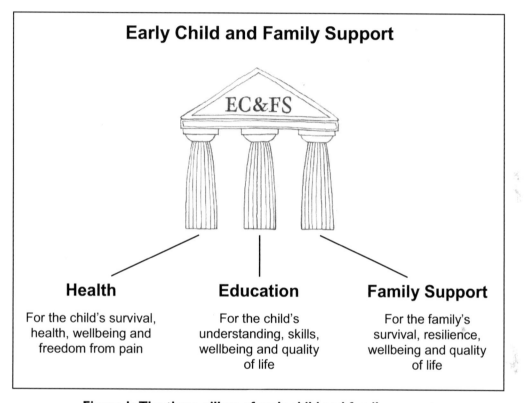

Figure 1: The three pillars of early child and family support

2

Health: The first pillar of early child and family support

For some babies and infants who have very special needs, the focus of support will need to be for a time on survival, health and freedom from pain. This work, by practitioners in hospital, children's hospice, community or all three, will be predominantly in the medical mode involving doctors, nurses and others. Relevant family support, when it is available, will include addressing the emotional needs of parents and family members, practical and financial arrangements for parents to spend as much time with their child as possible and plans for meeting the child's medical needs at home after discharge from hospital. This might require hospital-at-home provision.

When a young child's health is in crisis, short or long term, with many doctors and nurses involved, parents might wish for a TAC approach to build a whole picture of the situation and agree a unified and coherent response. In my experience, this is more likely to be achievable in a children's hospice than in a general hospital where the number of people involved and the busy medical atmosphere do not easily lend themselves to regular TAC meetings. Doctors and nurses' shift systems only add to the problems of getting relevant people together at the same time and place.

However, in these stressful times, a nurse, health visitor or social worker who can take on the role of keyworker will be of great benefit to parents to help them absorb all the information that is given them and to respond to it. This important role can include harmonising all hospital, hospice and community supports as far as possible into a child and family-centred whole. The keyworker becomes one familiar trusted person to rely on while other practitioners must inevitably come and go.

I am not qualified to discuss health issues in any depth. This book is concerned with babies and infants who have very special needs but who are not at this extreme level of dominant health need. While health and freedom from pain remain as ever-present concerns, the children and parents I am considering in this book are ready for some planned focus on the emergence of new understanding and skills.

This must be a matter of balanced judgement by everyone around the baby or infant. I have seen many cases of the health focus being so dominant, that the new child is viewed only as a patient who needs treatment and nothing more. This approach persisting in the medium and longer term can endanger child-parent attachment, deny the baby or infant his or her childhood and stifle the emergence of understanding and skills. Sometimes parents can see this situation clearly and will do all they can to be present for their new child with relationship, reassurance, sensory stimulation and first baby games. There is much more understanding now of how important this is even for babies in incubators in intensive care. Education starts at the beginning of life for every child and there is no time when child-parent attachment and quality of life of the new child and family can be ignored.

3

Education: The second pillar of early child and family support

This chapter has four sections:

1. Babies and infants as whole beings
2. The emergence of understanding and skills in babies and infants
3. Joined-up working
4. Summary

1. Babies and infants as whole beings

Children, with or without special needs, have a right to be respected and treated as whole beings who bring all of their understanding and skills into each of their activities. An infant playing on the floor with a ball in the company of a parent, sibling or playmate functions as a whole being because it is the only way they can be. The child is using skills in posture, movement, dexterity, seeing, listening and understanding. They might be remembering yesterday's game. They might be excitedly trying to reach the ball so they can pass it to a playmate. This is an infant's 'global' or whole-child activity. It is happening in all natural baby and infant behaviour and is reflected in complex interconnected neurological networks – networks that strengthen as activities that are relevant to the child are practised and repeated.

Each baby and infant's understanding, communication, emotions, and movement are all happening at the same time in the natural activities of dressing and undressing, mealtimes, play, etc. In these activities, each facet of child functioning depends on the others and each supports the others. As an example, we can think of a baby lying in a cot seeing a bauble hanging within reach. The first contacts between hands and bauble might happen accidentally from random movements. If the baby notices the bauble moving after she has touched it, then, in the coming hours, days, weeks, months or years, contact can become less random and more purposeful. The baby's hands and eyes gradually improve how they work together in this pleasurable activity. In this first learning or education arms, hands, eyes, attention, interest, intention, effort and emotions are all involved. If the bauble has a rattle inside, then ears are involved too. If an encouraging parent is nearby, then there will be the additional factors of relationship and encouragement.

But this interconnected and interdependent global functioning is not commonly recognised in traditional approaches to babies and infants who have very special needs. In the world of childhood disability, some practitioners are trained to focus on a single aspect of child development, for instance communication or movement. This narrow focus gives rise to deep understanding and skills. But, also, it has led to the dangerous professional myth that to support learning in infants who have a multifaceted condition, we can work on separate bits as though they were not interconnected parts of the whole child. This does no favours to child or family and does not reflect how first learning happens in natural whole-child activity. Systems theory can help us move away from this damaging fragmented approach.

Systems theory, sometimes called systems thinking, can help us understand babies and young children who have very special needs and then plan effective interventions to support their learning. A 'system' is an entity within which separate parts are connected together in such a way that the resulting system has new characteristics and can perform a particular function. For example, molecules join together to make cells, cells make organs and organs make bodies – yours and mine. Similarly, pedals, saddle, wheels and other bits make a bike we can ride to work. We can see that when simpler things join together in the right way they create new entities with characteristics the separate parts did not have. You cannot ride to work on a sack full of bicycle parts. Your body and mine, with all internal organs interconnected, can do endlessly amazing things. Systems theory shows us that new characteristics and potentials emerge when separate parts are joined together in a particular way.

I have argued already that in typically developing babies and infants, abilities with hands, balance, movement, eyes, ears all join together in such natural activities as playing, eating, drinking and managing clothes. New understanding and skills cannot emerge without this joining together. The baby touching the bauble described earlier was joining movement skills, posture skills and vision skills to achieve hand-eye co-ordination.

But can we also apply systems thinking to a new child's separate diagnoses of, for example, cerebral palsy, sensory deficits and learning difficulties? I argue that we should. We should think of them joining together as a system when we are considering how a young child acquires new understanding and skills. In which case, for each child a single unique multifaceted condition emerges in which the diagnosed elements or impairments interconnect with each other as the child plays and learns. The result are new characteristics that are not present in children who have any of those conditions singly. No two infants can have the same multifaceted condition – each must be valued, respected and treated as a unique child.

Systems thinking can take us even further in pursuit of effective early child and family support. The theory suggests that when the main people supporting a baby or infant who has very special needs join their separate interventions together in the right way, they, as practitioners or parents, will develop new understanding and skills. Collective competence emerges from this joining together – a major element of the TAC approach.[4]

---

[4] Limbrick, P. (2019) *Zen in care and support for new children who have disabilities.* http://www.tacinterconnections.com/index.php/allnews/ developmentsintreatment/3085-zen-in-care-and-support-for-new-children-who-have -disabilities

2. The emergence of understanding and skills in babies and infants

In traditional early childhood intervention, practitioners often talk of a young child's 'development and learning' and I have used the phrase myself earlier in this book. I think this phrase needs clarifying so we can see if it is still useful in 21st century early child and family support for babies and infants who have very special needs.

We can think of development as a process that continues as we grow older and learning as the knowledge, understanding and skills we accumulate dependent on what we experience in our family, school and culture. As an example, teenagers can learn chemistry, carpentry and cookery at the same time as they are developing biologically, socially and emotionally in puberty. Most babies and young children will go through the infant development stages of sitting, crawling and standing and then put the development to good use when they learn where the biscuit tin is kept. Obviously, development and learning are interconnected and interdependent in all of us.

In the cultures I know of, typically developing babies and infants are not taught how to crawl, stand or walk. Instead, these skills are left, more or less, to develop naturally – usually with encouragement and praise. But when a child has very special needs, some basic skills, for instance in posture, movement, use of hands and communication, will be directly supported or taught by early childhood practitioners rather than being left to develop naturally without help (or perhaps not develop at all). So, the distinction between development and learning become less useful. A better phrase is 'the emergence of relevant understanding and skills'. This phrase brings together understanding and skills that emerge with or without planned therapy or teaching.

It is well understood that young children learn through play. When we watch infants playing, we see them gaining understanding of their bodies and of the space around them. They become more skilful in moving, watching, listening and planning. They understand more and more about the children they are playing with and the adults watching over them. Their ability to communicate improves as they express frustration, success and pleasure. They learn how to ask for what they want, how to respond to requests made to them and how to work things out when their ideas conflict with others. They learn that actions have consequences.

We can see in our own lives and families that this emergence of relevant understanding and skills is a lifetime project. But my experience shows me that a new child's learning does not wait for infant play activity. It begins much earlier in babyhood during, for instance, feeding, nappy changing and bathing. Watching, listening, feeling and relating are happening at the breast or bottle. While being dressed and undressed babies are developing a first awareness of parts of the body, about the feel and smell of items of clothing and about changing position, feeling comfortable, managing balance, how to help (or not). In the rough and tumble of baby games with an energetic parent there is fear, excitement, moving through space and learning how to ask for more. At family mealtimes there is learning about routines, foods, waiting for one's turn, and being with the family – and sometimes not being the most important person in it.

So, we can extend important first learning back to babyhood and, if we wish, further back into the womb. In my thinking, learning or 'education' in which relevant understanding and skills emerge under appropriate conditions, is a continuing process that starts at the very beginning of life.

When we consider the vast store of relevant understanding and skills that is built up during a new child's first couple of years, we can see that it emerges:

- under the care of parents and other family members
- in the family home and other safe and familiar places
- in the natural activities of feeding, dressing routines, socialising, play, etc

In families all around the world this first learning happens without lessons or programmes. Understanding and skills emerge and grow during family activity in the domestic scene with the child feeling cared for, enjoyed, valued, relaxed and safe. In this book I am suggesting interventions for babies and infants who have very special needs can follow this natural approach to their first learning. Following the logic of the TAC approach, this must be a collective effort with joined-up working.

3. Joined-up working

TAC is the forum for practitioners and parents around the child to join their work together instead of keeping their approaches separate. This can be called joined-up working, joint working, integrated working or just integration. This whole-child approach to support the emergence of understanding and skills comes in progressive stages and each TAC (practitioners <u>and</u> parents, remember) decides how much joining up is appropriate for the child at the time. The stages for joint working in the TAC approach are listed in *Early Childhood Intervention without Tears*[5] as:

- Practitioners and parents sharing information
- Practitioners and parents supporting each other
- Integration of separate programmes into a whole approach
- Agreement that practitioners can work either directly or indirectly
- Agreeing a primary interventionist

The first two stages, in my view, are essential. Failing to achieve these first basic levels of joined-up working will be a serious disservice to the child, family and practitioners. The three remaining stages are applied in response to the individual needs and situation of each unique child and family. They are best thought of as approaches that can be configured to make a whole and coherent pattern of effective early child and family support.

---

[5] Limbrick, P. (2017) *Early Childhood Intervention without Tears: Improved support for infants with disabilities and their families.* Clifford: Interconnections
The stages of joint working described in *Early Childhood Intervention without Tears* are listed in the Appendix, p 98.

I am going to discuss these approaches to joint working now under just two headings:

- Sharing information and supporting each other's work
- Supporting parents in natural baby and infant activities

Sharing information and supporting each other's work

Joined-up working at this basic level means parent and practitioners in the TAC meetings tell each other what their approaches and methods are and what outcomes they are aiming for. Sharing in this way might bring to light some approaches that do not really fit together and some duplications in which two people are doing much the same thing. These issues are then easily resolved.

Once TAC members know what each other is doing, everyone takes what they can from the other's work. In this way, everyone starts using the same communication approach, the same floor or seating positions and the same sort of prompts and encouragements. The parental contribution to this is just as important as the practitioners' because they already know so much more about their child. From this level of joined-up working the child gets a consistent approach from everyone and increased opportunities to practice signs, words, positions, movements, use of hands, etc.

Supporting parents in natural baby and infant activities

This level of integrated or joined-up working in a TAC system learns from how new understanding and skills emerge for typically-developing babies and infants at home in the family setting. The task for each child's TAC is to translate what most parents do naturally into what practitioners and parents can do together when the child has very special needs. The underlying principle is for practitioners to sensitively support parents in their role of bringing up their child.

The topics to be discussed here are:

- Collective competence
- Working directly or indirectly

- Primary interventionists
- Focusing on natural activities in the family setting
- New neurological networks

Collective competence

This is achieved in a child's TAC when everyone learns from each other. It emerges from the joining together of each person's separate understanding and skills. As an example, we can think again of a baby learning to reach and touch a suspended bauble. For this example we can envisage a baby boy who has difficulties in arm and hand movement combined with limited vision – perhaps with diagnoses of cerebral palsy and vision impairment. His parents are sure he can sometimes see the bauble and have asked their practitioners to help them teach him to touch it. The parents sense this is what their baby wants to do.

To help in this, practitioners must bring together their professional knowledge about how children can be helped to overcome posture and movement difficulties and about how children can make maximum use of limited vision. We must then add parents' all-round knowledge about their baby boy's likes and dislikes, interests, favourite toys, times of wakefulness, moods, etc. All of this knowledge is held by separate people, in this example parents, physiotherapist and teacher of vision impaired children, so there must be a process of bringing it all together to help the baby master this multifaceted task. In fact, there is one more person involved in this collective competence because the child brings their present understanding and skills into the mix.

It is a straightforward, uncomplicated and obvious TAC process for this small team of people to share their separate understanding and skills with each other and to discuss ways forward. From this joining up emerges collective competence. Then there needs to be only one person spending time at the side of the cot helping the baby instead of three or four!

This very basic joint working that creates collective competence is, in my view, appropriate generally in support of parents of babies and infants who have a multifaceted condition. If the parents and practitioners around the baby boy persisted in keeping their work separate from each other, there could be no whole view of the baby's present abilities nor a whole approach to the bauble-reaching task (game). How ridiculous it would be to have all these adults around the boy's cot on a regular basis with their separate approaches and programmes! Sad to say, this fragmented approach is common in traditional early childhood intervention.

TAC creates a unique and integrated multifaceted action plan for each baby or infant who has a unique multifaceted condition. As the child's practitioners and parents work closely together in honest, trusting and respectful relationships they achieve collective competence which can help the baby or infant acquire new understanding and skills in the natural activities of babyhood and infancy. This is a common-sense alternative to treating a child in bits.

Collective competence around the baby boy above means that parents, vision impairment teacher and physiotherapist become equally know-ledgeable and competent to help the child learn to reach and touch the bauble. In most cases, it will be the parents who devote most time to this natural baby/infant activity with the two practitioners available to help again when necessary.

We can see that achieving collective competence around babies and infants who have a multifaceted condition offers practitioners the possibility of changing their work patterns with the young children on their case list. This brings direct benefit for the new child, the family and the practitioners in the TAC as described in the next section.

Working directly or indirectly

Joint working in TAC offers practitioners two ways of working with the child: directly or indirectly. This creates flexibility in how busy practitioners use their time with the children on their case list. In direct work, a teacher, therapist or psychologist, for example, works with the child in clinic, at the child's home or elsewhere on a particular programme. Working indirectly, the other option, means that one practitioner hands over some part of their work for another person or persons to do in their place for an agreed period. There is one person who hands over and one or more people who take on some of that person's work. In our example above, it was natural for the baby boy's parents to take on the direct work (play).

Working indirectly is not a new idea. Practitioners are accustomed to showing parents what they can do as 'homework' and to showing staff members in nurseries and schools what they can do to promote a child's new understanding and skills in, for instance, movement or communication. But indirect working needs careful planning. Each of the practitioners in a child's TAC must come to their own professional decision about the parts of their work they can hand over to another and which parts they must keep for themselves, perhaps for the time being. The other considerations in indirect working include establishing that the people taking on the work are competent to do so, have the necessary time, resources and space, and can have refreshers when they feel the need.

In traditional approaches, both the new child and the parents can be overwhelmed and overloaded with too many separate practitioners, programmes and venues to get to. Indirect working, in which one or more practitioners for an agreed period move into the background, takes pressure off new children, parents and professional teams.

Primary Interventionists

Indirect working in TAC can mean that just one practitioner is supported to work directly with a child and parent while others for an agreed period take more of a back seat. This practitioner can be called the primary interventionist. This must be a TAC decision made in the best interests of the individual child and family.

This way of working is described in *Primary Interventionists in the Team Around the Child Approach*. In this essay there is an example of a child's TAC using film to keep TAC members informed about the child's activities. Film can establish the child's skills at the beginning and show progress as the work proceeds. Film is a great asset in indirect working to support a primary interventionist.

The primary interventionist can only function with the full support of other TAC members. No practitioner can 'go it alone' in offering a whole approach to a child who has a multifaceted condition. No practitioner has sufficient all-round skills for this.

The primary interventionist model can help protect the child's and parents' psychological wellbeing, attachment between the infant and parents, and quality of life for the child and family. Here is an extract from the essay answering the question, 'Who or what is a primary interventionist?':

Within the TAC approach, primary interventionists are not a defining feature.
They are an option for a TAC to adopt if it is felt necessary for the child and

family. A primary interventionist is the person chosen in TAC discussion to work with a child and family for a period of time when TAC members (remember parents are fully involved) feel there should only be one person offering most of the direct support. The reasons for coming to this decision include the following:

1. *The baby or infant does not have the capacity at this time to relate comfortably to a number of interventionists or to accept being handled by them. This can be true for all new babies and for babies and infants who have sensory impairment or anxiety, fear of strangers and a general apprehension about the world they find themselves in.*

2. *The parent or parents do not have the capacity at this time to relate comfortably to a number of interventionists or to develop effective working relationships with them. It is felt the regular calm threesome or foursome of parent(s), infant and interventionist will provide the best conditions to support attachment between parent(s) and child.*

3. *It is felt the child will have the optimum chance of success in each chosen learning task when supported by a single early interventionist who can integrate all facets of infant activity including communication, movement, vision, hearing and understanding.*

4. *It is felt parents needing support in helping their child learn basic baby and infant skills (for instance baby games, playing with toys, moving around the room, managing first undressing skills, using a spoon and cup) will have optimum chance of increasing their confidence, competence and self-esteem when they are regularly supported by just one person they get on well with and trust.[6]*

The essay explains that the primary interventionist model can be the first TAC option for supporting parents with their new baby or it can be a

---

[6] Limbrick, P. (2018) *Primary Interventionists in the TAC Approach: A guide for managers and practitioners supporting families whose baby or infant has a multifaceted condition.* Clifford: Interconnections, pp 20-21.

remedy when child and/or parents become, or are likely to become, over-whelmed with too many people and too much going on.

Focusing on natural activities in the family setting

As mentioned earlier in the book, one of my aims is to describe how far interventions for learning can focus on natural daily activities when the baby or infant has a multifaceted condition. Moving in this direction would mean a child has fewer sessions for 'physiotherapy' or 'speech and language therapy' and, instead, more support in, for instance, eating and drinking, undressing and dressing, or moving purposefully around the room or house – but involving the same TAC members. As far as possible this work will begin in the family home and will be in support of parents in their task of bringing up their child. In this approach, interventions might well focus on a part of the child's day that parents are finding most challenging, perhaps to do with washing, mealtimes or bedtime.

When moving in this way from discipline-specific goals set by the child's practitioners towards natural activities in response to parents' concerns or aspirations, the people in the child's TAC will need to share their knowledge and expertise about how babies and infants enhance their skills in each chosen activity – as with the baby boy and the bauble.

In this shift of approaches, we can take encouragement from the physiotherapist, Sophie Levitt. In her book *Basic Abilities: A whole approach*[7], she describes in detail how parents of young children who have disabilities can build therapy into their daily activities. She strongly suggests parents should refer to their child's practitioners as necessary.

Sophie divides baby and infant development into four stages; 0-6 months, 6-12 months, 1-2 years and 2-3 years. She groups daily activities as: eating and drinking; washing; dressing, toileting; play; moving from place to place. Because of her whole-child mindset, within each daily activity at each stage of development, she discusses how to help the child under the

---

[7] Levitt, S. (1994) *Basic Abilities: A whole approach.* UK: Souvenir Press

headings: controlling posture and movement, using hands, looking, listening, sensing, communicating, understanding.

To give the flavour of the book, here are four examples of Sophie's suggestions to parents. I have taken one from each of her four stages of development. Each example is paraphrased and abbreviated.

1. To promote listening in the washing activity, amuse the child with songs, different tones of voice and gentle, interesting sounds such as water and sounds from the washing actions. Encourage the child to look at your face or hands moving and making a noise in front, to each side, above and below the child.

2. To promote use of hands in the dressing activity, encourage the child to reach, touch and grasp items of clothing as well as their feet, toes, opposite arm and leg – as the child will later use these actions for dressing. Guide the child to slide large rings of clothing material, bangles or cardboard along their arms or legs. Encourage the child to pass a sock from hand to hand, to hold it with both hands and to drop it and find it with help.

3. To promote communication in eating and drinking activity at this stage when the child might understand more natural gestures, signs and words, the child may be shown some gestures or special signs with words to precede 'eating' or 'drinking'. The child may be able to say what is 'hot' or 'cold', 'give me', 'no', 'yes', 'thank you' or to ask for more. Development of communication (and speech) varies widely in individuals.

4. For controlling posture and moving in play activity, play games with the child which encourage him to climb into a box, on top of chairs and tables and underneath and behind furniture. In this way the child comes to realise how the size of their body fits into things. Later the child can understand the words meaning 'inside', 'outside', 'on top', 'underneath', 'behind' once the child is able to do these things.

In Sophie Levitt's whole approach, parents are helping their child in natural activities using what they already know and have learned from their child's practitioners and then referring back to them as necessary. The baby or infant in this natural approach has increased opportunities to develop and practise new understanding and skills. The child's efforts now have a purpose. Whether the activity is to do with washing, moving or playing, the baby or infant is learning about starting with an intention, focusing on a task, working through the various steps of the activity and then having some sense of completion, understanding and perhaps satisfaction at the end.

In the section on dressing in Sophie's book, there is a picture of a child being supported to stand to a chest of drawers where the clothes are kept. For a child who needs regular practice to stand with support, this is a wonderful opportunity to make the exercise meaningful by using the time to explore the clothes in the drawer and for a conversation about what they are called and what colour they are. To promote autonomy, the child can be asked what they want to wear that day and may help taking those things out of the drawer. I am sure that for many typically developing children, none of this would be unusual.

Parents just do what parents do naturally without having to try to be a 'therapist' in Sophie's child and parent-friendly approach and the baby or infant is less subject to unnatural discipline-specific programmes. A child's TAC can decide to use this approach and move towards promoting new understanding and skills in natural activities – breaking away, as appropriate, from discipline-specific goals.

Each natural baby or infant activity is multifaceted. For instance, undressing and dressing has many facets including some awareness and understanding about body parts and items of clothing, practice of balance in changing postures, moving limbs, feeling textures, smelling materials, looking, grasping parts of clothing, listening to instructions, responding to encouragement, wanting to be helpful, choosing clothes, and a feeling of satisfaction with a new achievement.

Another example is managing drinks at mealtime. The following is a list of some facets to be considered when planning support for parents who want to help their baby or infant gain understanding and skills in the activity of taking a drink from a cup while sitting at a tray or table:

- Seating arrangement and sitting posture to facilitate control of head, arm(s) and hand(s)
- Tray or table, non-slip table mat
- Type of cup and handle(s)
- Present hand skills and ability to use hands and eyes together
- Position of parent who is helping the child at the table
- Appropriate two-way communication with child about wanting a drink
- The child's listening, vision and attention skills
- Preferences for type of drink and necessary thickness and quantity in the cup
- Understanding, acceptance, memory and motivation for the routine of sitting at the table and having a drink
- Choosing which small steps to focus on in the sequence of seeing, reaching, grasping, lifting cup to lips
- Managing cup at lips, taking liquid, swallowing
- Reverse sequence to put cup back on table and release grasp
- How and when to assist, prompt and praise

Each natural baby and infant activity will have a similar list of facets or components. Some children will need a more detailed approach than others. For babies and infants who have very special needs and a multifaceted condition, there will need to be careful discussion of each facet of whichever natural activity is being focussed on. It would not help a child in any task if, for instance, posture, communication or, especially, understanding were ignored. If support is mismanaged in this way, progress will be impeded and damage might be done. It becomes clear why a joined-up approach is essential to bring everyone's knowledge, understanding and skills together.

New neurological networks

The baby or infant's new understanding and new skills are mirrored in new neurological connections, pathways and networks. With practice, these new neurological patterns strengthen and become firmly established. Without practice, perhaps when the activity has no interest or relevance to the child, the neurological connections will not become established and will fade away. When a child learns to see and touch a bauble, there will not be separate neurological pathways for movement and for seeing. They will be fully integrated into the new neurological pattern for bauble touching. Just as flour, fat and sugar can no longer be found as separate items in pastry, so a child's separate diagnoses or impairments cannot be found in this new learning. And just as pastry has enjoyable new characteristics that emerge when parts are cooked together, so learning to see and touch a bauble is a multifaceted success story in which there are no disabilities.

4. Summary

In this chapter on education, the second pillar of early child and family support, I have discussed support for parents as they promote their child's new understanding and skills. I have suggested that we model the approach on how children do their first learning at home, within the family in natural daily activities. In this, the unambiguous role for practitioners is to support parents in their role of bringing up their children. The approach is sensitive to children and family members and is respectful of parents' rights and responsibilities.

Just as typically developing young children gradually increase their understanding and skills in their natural activities, so will infants who have very special needs. We can see that children being helped with drinking or managing clothes are learning and practising skills with posture, eyes, ears, hands and mouth. They are in relationship and communication with a parent and are increasing their understanding of the whole 'having a drink at the table' or 'dressing and undressing' situations.

Each natural activity brings a wealth of learning opportunities that overlap with and support other natural activities. The baby girl or boy with the bauble has emerging understanding and skills in the practicalities of posture, arm and hand movement and vision but is also learning about attention, intention, effort, responding to encouragement and all the fun of a new game. This new learning will be valuable in every other activity whether moving around the room, bath time, bedtime or playing on the floor. Importantly, in all of these activities, parents are learning how their new child learns best in terms of the general situation, time of day, encouragement, rewards, etc. This is valuable information.

There is a danger of practitioners approaching these natural activities from the wrong end. It is not a matter of taking practitioners' preferred discipline-specific development and learning goals and cleverly integrating them into natural activities. We must start at the other end with the chosen natural activity. When responding to parent's request for help, the process must start by observing the child's existing understanding and skills in the natural activity at home and then designing TAC support for further learning. In effective early child and family support, everyone's thinking moves from narrow discipline-specific goals towards rich and relevant natural activity.

If this whole-child thinking feels strange, it might be because we are so used to the idea of compartmentalised areas of infant development leading to compartmentalised therapy and teaching. Getting back to the singular, back to the whole interconnected child with a single unique multifaceted condition can seem like a revolution when it is no such thing. In the end, it just means getting back to how most parents think about and treat their children. I must be clear, though, that the term 'multifaceted condition' applies only when we are thinking about education. I am sure it is not such a useful concept for physicians and surgeons.

It is relevant in the TAC approach to reconsider the roles of prac- titioners designated as therapists and teachers. In my view, the distinction between therapy and education breaks down in support for babies and infants who have a multifaceted condition. Helping a child's visually directed reaching (the baby and the bauble again), managing a cup and drink at mealtime and getting clothes on and off each have elements of what is traditionally called therapy and what is traditionally called teaching. These natural whole-child skills do not respect traditional child development categories or professional disciplines. The integrated TAC approach to support parents as they bring up their new children moves beyond unhelpful divisions between education and therapy just as it moves beyond distinctions between development and learning.

In modern early child and family support, the common-sense approach focusing on natural family activities can become the core of support for a child's gradually emerging new understanding and skills. While I have focused on helping parents with their child at home, many parents will choose sooner or later to use mother & baby groups, playgroups, children's centres and nurseries. In these settings, parents can support each other and escape the confines of the home while the child is exploring a wider social world. The understanding and skills the baby or infant is acquiring at home will be equally relevant in this expanded social scene.

I have spoken about how babies and young children learn as though I know all about it. What I know I have learned from working with new children and their families. By now, I have worked with enough children to realise that how they learn is essentially a mystery. I am in awe of that mystery and in awe of young children I have known who have acquired understanding and skills against all the odds.

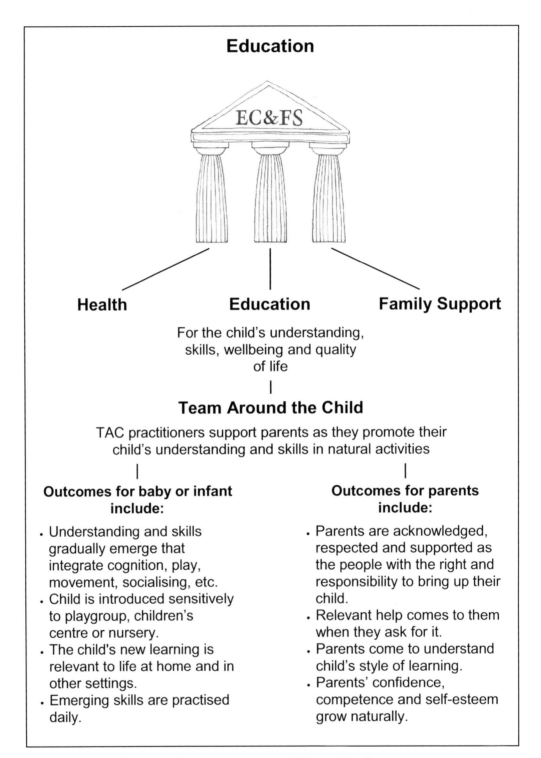

Education

EC&FS

Health   Education   Family Support

For the child's understanding,
skills, wellbeing and quality
of life

Team Around the Child

TAC practitioners support parents as they promote their
child's understanding and skills in natural activities

Outcomes for baby or infant include:

- Understanding and skills gradually emerge that integrate cognition, play, movement, socialising, etc.
- Child is introduced sensitively to playgroup, children's centre or nursery.
- The child's new learning is relevant to life at home and in other settings.
- Emerging skills are practised daily.

Outcomes for parents include:

- Parents are acknowledged, respected and supported as the people with the right and responsibility to bring up their child.
- Relevant help comes to them when they ask for it.
- Parents come to understand child's style of learning.
- Parents' confidence, competence and self-esteem grow naturally.

Figure 2: Education in early child and family support

4

Family Support: The third pillar of early child and family support

The family, with its many traditional and modern variations in all countries, is accepted as the social structure for bringing up children. It follows that all sorts of families in all cultures in every country are accepted as being strong enough with parents who are up to the task. Inevitably, there is much variation in this. Adults differ in their parenting skills. All families go through testing times and some meet crises when support from outside the family is welcome – when sought. Support should do nothing to take away the family's strength, undermine parents or detract from the family's drive to get back on track. Most families I have known with children who have very special needs get through the most challenging times to find a new liveable family life. In this process over months or years, the new child, who at first brought so much worry, becomes a loved and not-so-exclusively-special member of the family and a valued pupil in a nursery or school.

I hope readers have perceived in the chapters so far, a concern for the general wellbeing and quality of life of children who have very special needs and of their families that goes far beyond the concerns of traditional therapy and education. In the countries I know of, there is a prevailing assumption that parents of these babies and young children must resign themselves to being stressed and exhausted much of the time. Then practitioners are rarely surprised to hear that a parental relationship has failed or that a mother or father or both are taking antidepressants. Parents who have a practitioner they trust might confide in them that they are at the end of their tether and perhaps harbouring very dark thoughts about ways out of the situation. Some parents have told me they had contemplated suicide before effective support was in place and local newspapers from time to time relate very tragic stories about parents of children who have very special needs killing themselves. It is my experience that parents in these extreme situations are angry, frustrated and despairing about the inadequacy of support for their child, not about their child's special needs.

Managers and practitioners in support agencies should not assume that stress, exhaustion and deep frustration are inevitable. Very often they have causes to which there are practical solutions. This book suggests many antidotes, the first step of which can be active listening in a relationship marked by genuine human concern, kindness, respect and trust. In up-to-date early child and family support, agencies and their practitioners will consider the situation and quality of life of the whole family. This must include siblings, grandparents and, of course, the baby or young child who has very special needs.

In traditional services, family support can be absent or minimal, so it is worth reminding ourselves why it is the essential third pillar of effective early child and family support. My reasons include:

- New families can be suffering severe emotional stress and physical exhaustion. Timely support can help the family survive and resist the forces that might cause two parents to separate.
- The stronger the family is, the better it is able to support the baby or infant who has very special needs and any siblings. This includes favourable conditions for child-parent attachment.
- Effective support for new parents can build resilience to help the family meet the inevitable challenges during the coming years as the child goes through school and enters adulthood.

When there is a new child who has very special needs, the family's needs are different from the child's needs. While the child needs effective health and education support, the family might need varied support from a wide range of agencies and practitioners. The help needed can be for:

- caring for and bringing up the child
- adjusting to the new conditions
- maintaining a quality of life

Help in caring for and bringing up the child

Many parents will have a lot to learn about managing symptoms, giving medications and using medical equipment at home. They might need help in providing good conditions for infant-parent attachment. They might need support in promoting the child's new understanding and skills and in nurturing their quality of life.

When a new nursing mother of any child seeks help in baby-care tasks, she can turn to a more experienced family member, friend, doula or nurse – at home or in hospital. In most cases this will be one woman helping another. When a baby has very special needs, new parents might seek help in feeding, cuddling, handling the baby for changes, bathing and dressing, and perhaps in first rhymes and baby games. This help might come from a nurse, another practitioner or another parent with experience of babies with these needs.

This sort of help is straightforward, uncomplicated and entirely natural. In my view, when it is done well, it offers a valuable guide for agencies and practitioners supporting parents of babies and young children who have very special needs in the longer term. The relevant features of this uncomplicated approach include the following:

- Help is given when asked for and it comes from one person the parent or parents trust enough to approach for help.
- The helper is sensitive and respectful and has a dual concern – for the parent(s) and for the infant.
- Parents' role in bringing up their child is acknowledged.

- The helper knows more than the parents do at this time about this particular issue.
- With sensitive support, parents become more knowledgeable and competent and therefore have reduced stress and anxiety and increased dignity and self-esteem.
- Parents are given the best possible start for helping their child's new understanding and skills during the pre-school years.
- The infant has good conditions for first learning with reduced anxiety and stress as parents become more relaxed and sure of themselves.

Early childhood intervention agencies would do well to aspire to this straightforward mode of support in which infant, parent and practitioner work as a threesome – or a foursome if two parents are involved. This approach is in stark contrast to the chaos of multiple practitioners and programmes that can chip away at a child and family's strength and quality of life.

Adjusting to the new conditions

Many needs can arise for parents and other close family members as direct consequences of the baby or infant's very special needs. A short list can include help for:

- managing excessive tiredness, anxiety, stress, depression and guilt
- maintaining relationships within the family
- sleep deprivation
- housing issues, claiming benefits and debt management
- continuing or returning to studies
- continuing or returning to work
- organising family outings and holidays
- getting short breaks from the caring role to 'recharge batteries'.

Maintaining a quality of life

The family as a whole might need support in achieving and maintaining a quality of life. This section considers some needs of siblings, grandparents, the new child with very special needs and lastly, the parent or parents.

There can be direct challenges to the quality of life for brothers and sisters whether they are older or younger than the young child who has very special needs. These can include the following:

- Picking up their parents' anxieties
- Harbouring their own worries, hopes, anxieties, frustrations and feelings of guilt
- Parents being less available to them
- Losing sleep and doing less well at school
- Family outings and holidays being curtailed
- Sport and leisure activities after school or at weekends becoming impossible
- Friends falling away as they can no longer be invited home
- Gradually taking on the role of a young carer – whether they or their parents want this to happen

Grandparents, who might or might not live in the vicinity, are likely to have their own emotional response to the grandchild who has special needs as well as to their son or daughter and their partners. This is a double concern. They might decide to get fully involved and take on a new caring role in their later years or be content to stay in the background. Grandparents living close enough might opt to become part-time carers or baby-sitters to help the parents get some time off. Some grandparents might want to do this but hold back because they are not sure they will cope with the situations that might arise. When practitioners are made aware of this, they can organise some sessions to answer questions and show a grandparent what they need to know. It is likely that many grandparents will value a listening ear and emotional support from time to time.

Babies and infants who have very special needs will surely have challenges to their quality of life. They might have situations and routines imposed on them that are very different from those of typically developing infants. Being aware of this does not mean the child will no longer have to undergo some unpleasant procedures and unwelcome situations, but it can mean the infant's quality of life is given full importance and brought into action planning. Perhaps this comes more naturally to parents than to many practitioners. The rule here that we must respect is that all children are deserving of respect and have rights, special needs or not. The challenges to an infant's quality of life can include the following:

- Ongoing pain or discomfort
- Fearful and insecure mental states
- Inadequate nutrition and hunger
- Sleep deprivation
- Impeded attachment
- Interrupted routines for feeding, daytime sleeps, play, etc
- Being frequently handled by a number of non-family adults who might expect the child to want to relate to them
- Too few opportunities to just be a baby or an infant at home doing what babies and infants do naturally
- Having parents who are rarely relaxed with a calm mind and time to 'just be' with them

There are many factors influencing the quality of life of the parents of a baby or infant who has very special needs and these are woven through all parts of this book. While I can list some of them, I would not attempt to put them in priority order. My short list of contributory factors to parents' quality of life would include self-esteem and self-respect, good relationships within the close family, seeing the baby or infant free of health crises and pain, watching the infant acquire new understanding and skills, feeling the other children in the family are enjoying a decent childhood and progressing well at school – and then some relief from persistent sleep deprivation, exhaustion and negative emotional states.

Parents might discover that the arrival of a new child who has very special needs changes all aspects of the life of their family. Their previous work and study patterns, socialising, leisure activity, holidays, finances and plans for the future can be temporarily thrown into turmoil. Parents can come to feel they are no longer in control of the family's wellbeing.

It is not unusual for parents and other family members to re-evaluate spiritual beliefs and basic attitudes to life. Of course, families are unique and nothing can be assumed. I have seen some families that fail to survive or get stuck in negative attitudes. In other families I have seen parents begin a whole new life of supporting other new parents through difficult times. I have seen many parents emerge from the turmoil with new insights about humanity and our responsibility as human beings to help each other. Generalising about this will not be helpful, but I am sure that as parents work to get their family back on track, having someone with whom to discuss the issues will be helpful. Such discussions can help parents see their situation more clearly and can explore creative ways forward.

Practitioners offering family support must keep in mind that parents and some grandparents and siblings are likely to be caring for the child for many years, perhaps decades into the future. It is salutary for all early childhood practitioners to remember that they are probably with the family for a relatively short period of time. A practitioner might have helped lay good foundations even though the family in years to come might not remember their name or what they did.

The exceptions to this come when a child does not live beyond the first days, weeks, months or years. I have known many infants who have died, and I know of nothing sadder, but it is still valid to talk of family strength, about a family's struggle to keep functioning and about a possible need for relevant support that is available at the time when it is asked for. In many countries there are organisations to help and these include children's hospices whose practitioners might be with a family on this heart-breaking journey.

Typically, early childhood intervention agencies and practitioners in medical and educational settings do not have the resources to be fully effective in supporting families. Some practitioners will be aware that parents have emotional needs and will try to respond with kindness and sympathy. Whether they have time or skills to be skilled listeners and help in other ways will depend on the particular situation. The long list in the Appendix[8] shows the very many issues, questions and anxieties that might be on a parent's mind whenever they meet a new practitioner. While the parent hopes for help, the list goes far beyond the understanding and skills of any individual practitioner the parent will encounter. In an early child and family support system, a question or dilemma posed to one practitioner should be considered as posed to the whole system – within the limits of the confidentiality agreement between the parent and practitioner or agency.

Effective family support will recruit the expertise, efforts and resources of a wide range of agencies and practitioners. A TAC keyworker can support family members in locating appropriate agencies and practitioners for their particular needs but, for reasons of sensitivity and confidentiality, many of the issues would not be appropriate for discussion in TAC meetings. Whoever comes along to offer family support must start by listening to the family member's situation and needs. There is no room for assumptions in this. Issues must be explored fully and then ways forward discussed, leaving the family member in control at all times.

---

[8] 'Questions a parent might need answers to.' Appendix p 95.

5

Evaluating early child and family support

The support offered to babies and infants who have very special needs varies greatly. At the least effective end of the range, in some parts of the UK a child will be seen by just one or two practitioners providing short periods of support during the pre-school years. For children in other parts there can be a well-organised early childhood intervention system involving therapists, teachers and family support workers all co-operating to meet child and family needs during the first years. A great deal of information has been collected during recent decades from many countries about what babies and infants who have very special needs and their families might need, but there are very few examples of well-organised local systems in my country. Sadly, many parents have to fight for what their child and family needs with great cost to the child's wellbeing and to the family's peace of mind and quality of life.

Two groups of people need to be involved in evaluating local support in the pre-school years, firstly parents and then practitioners and their managers.

Practitioners and their managers first. Every practitioner working in an agency supporting babies and infants who have very special needs, whether in health, education or family support, must be confident that their work satisfies their personal, agency and professional standards. When it does not for some reason, it is an issue for discussion with colleagues, supervisor or agency management. Issues can arise because managers have concerns about a practitioner's performance or because a practitioner feels they are being asked to work in ways they are not comfortable with or competent in. With each child and family, practitioners must be confident they are able or enabled to do what their job description requires and that they are working within the initial agreement they, or their agency managers, have made with the parents.

Evaluation of early child and family support by a local agency must rely heavily on the parents' point of view and include support from all the agencies and practitioners around them. This all-embracing evaluation, which must include health, education and family support, is necessary because while one practitioner is providing a valued service they might be part of a disorganised and chaotic totality. While one agency is up to date, others might be stuck in unhelpful traditional attitudes. There might or might not be efforts for all agencies to work together in the TAC approach.

Out-dated agencies left over from the last century, while offering some elements of support, will leave children and families with significant unmet needs. For instance, families can be badly let down by agencies in a medical mode that cannot bring educational expertise to the child's learning or by agencies in an educational mode that cannot provide family support. Between the most out-dated and the most effective up-to-date early child and family support lies a wide range of approaches with varying capacities to genuinely listen to what parents need and to treat children with respect and sensitivity.

Part of this evaluation by parents can mean measuring the support the child and family are receiving, or have received, against what was offered or promised when the parents opted for a local service or services.

Potentially, a third set of people could be involved in evaluating early child and family support. These are those working in agencies charged with guiding, inspecting, monitoring and regulating public services.

"Hey, do you want to know what parents think of the support our children are getting?"

In my country, examples are NICE (National Institute for Health and Care Excellence)[9] and OFSTED (Office for Standards in Education)[10]. While NICE covers such medical topics as spina bifida and neonatal infection, it seems not to concern itself with more general care of new children who have disabilities or their families. OFSTED, as far as I am aware, is concerned with children who have childminders or are in children's centres, pre-schools and nurseries but not with babies and infants still at home.

This absence of guidance or monitoring leaves agencies and practitioners without a national structure to work within and it leaves parents with no official help when they want to appeal for effective, or more effective, early child and family support. With this absence of official concern, local agencies can be effective or ineffective, making their own independent decisions about what to offer. Babies and young children who have very

---

[9] NICE website: https://www.nice.org.uk/

[10] OFSTED website: https://www.gov.uk/government/organisations/ofsted

special needs are in no man's land until they enter some sort of childminding or educational provision outside the home. Of course, there are laws about how children in general should be treated and these apply to all children with or without special needs,

*

I have described a 21st century support system for babies and infants who have very special needs and their families. It might be helpful here to list the main features. The list can be used for agreeing support for a new family, guiding practitioners in their work and evaluating how successful the child and family support is or has been. The main features are as follows:

- Parents are recognised, acknowledged and supported as the people with the right to bring up their baby or young child and are treated with all respect and sensitivity.
- Agencies and their practitioners are available to provide relevant effective support when invited to do so.
- This support has three equally important strands: for the child's survival, health, wellbeing and freedom from pain; for the child's understanding and skills, wellbeing and quality of life; for the family's survival, resilience, wellbeing and quality of life. These are the three pillars of early child and family support: health, education and family support.
- The child is valued and respected, treated as a whole child and supported in enjoying the best possible quality of life with freedom from discomfort and pain as far as possible.
- Attachment between child and parents (and other family members) is a major consideration at all times.
- Support for the child's new understanding and skills happens primarily in the family home and then in other places the child is familiar with and feels secure in.
- Therapy and education approaches to support the baby or infant's learning are joined together as appropriate and focus on

56

the child's natural activities of play, socialising, mealtimes, managing clothes, bath time, etc.

- The number of practitioners offering regular direct support for the child's learning is kept to a minimum. This is to reduce tiredness and stress that infants and parents can suffer when there are too many appointments and too much going on.

- In some situations the number of practitioners can be reduced to a single primary interventionist for a period.

- The whole family is considered including siblings, grandparents and others thought of as 'family'. Efforts are made to meet their needs as far as possible. Quality of life is nurtured and the family is supported in getting back on track to a new version of normal family life when they are ready.

I do not advocate legal contracts between agencies and new parents. Also, it would be inappropriate for a practitioner to offer assurances to parents about what their baby or infant will achieve. But parents must be given some idea of what is on offer when they accept a support service. In my view, a modern early child and family support system should explain clearly to parents what they are offering, how they will work and what outcomes can be reasonably expected.

This can be in the form of an initial agreement or informal contract emerging from discussions between parents and support agencies and can be based on the above list. The following are just three examples of items for such an agreement written by the agency and given to the parents:

- We respect your right and responsibility to bring up your child. We will offer you support in this when asked.

- We will value and respect your child, treat them as a whole child and support you in giving them the best possible quality of life with freedom from discomfort and pain as far as possible.

- We will work with you to make sure support for your child is properly organised to reduce tiredness, stress and strain on your child and on yourselves as parent(s)

This abbreviated list needs to be extended to include other items from the list of main features above. When an agency or its practitioners and parents come to an initial agreement, the list should include items that relate to the individual child and family in their unique situation.

6

Humanity around babies and young children who have very special needs

The word 'humanity' is deliberately chosen for this chapter for its double meaning; firstly, a collection of people and secondly, the kindness of human beings. The collection of people around a baby or infant includes both children and adults and, amongst the adults, some who are family members and friends and others who are paid workers in public, private and voluntary agencies. Babies and infants who have very special needs are deserving of kindness from everyone they encounter and will perhaps in return help them become kinder people than they were before. This does happen.

I am going to discuss parents, other adult family members and practitioners together as people who have much in common with each other as human beings and who need to understand and get on with each other. All of these people have rich opportunities to bring their personality and humanity into their care for these babies and young children.

Let's start with a story. It is a made-up story that some early childhood practitioners tell new parents of babies and young children who have special needs. In this story, someone in the UK has booked a holiday in an exotic resort with sun-drenched beaches. The plane is forced to land in Holland instead and there this traveller must stay. At first, they are angry and disappointed but soon begin to explore and appreciate what Holland has to offer. After a time, they are happy to be in Holland and dream less often about the holiday they did not have.

The story suggests that parents who are disappointed because the perfect baby did not arrive will find themselves in a better situation if they just change their point of view. This does happen for very many parents, but it does not come quite so easily as in this story or as quickly. The potential to emerge from a dark place with new insights and wisdom is a human characteristic but it takes time and it needs patience and work. Much more is needed than the easy advice this story offers.

But the practitioner in the story has brought their humanity into their work and sees two situations in each family. Firstly, there is an infant who has special needs for wellbeing, health, development, learning and, perhaps, survival. Secondly, there is a parent or two parents (and probably other close family members) having to adjust to a life situation they had not expected, wanted or prepared for. Families differ in how they respond to this challenge, but, at first, there can be emotional turmoil with upset, anxiety, guilt and blame amongst other negative emotions. The 'being unhappy in Holland' phase can last for weeks, months or years and will bring some families down.

These negative states belong to parents, perhaps to grandparents, perhaps to siblings but not to the infant. Support agencies and the practitioners within them must recognise this dual situation – an infant with one set of needs and a family with another. The two sets of needs are interrelated but distinct.

I am going to discuss humanity in the care and support of these children under three headings::

- Relationships
- Negative mental states shared by parents and practitioners
- Becoming an advocate or champion

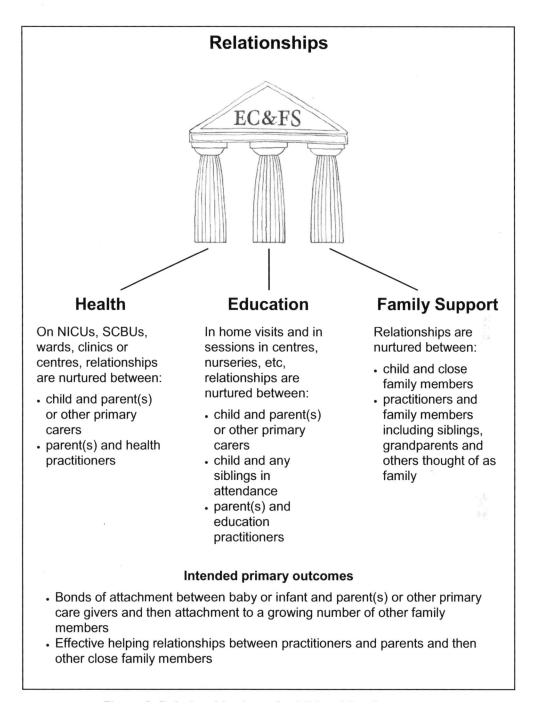

Relationships

EC&FS

Health

On NICUs, SCBUs, wards, clinics or centres, relationships are nurtured between:

- child and parent(s) or other primary carers
- parent(s) and health practitioners

Education

In home visits and in sessions in centres, nurseries, etc, relationships are nurtured between:

- child and parent(s) or other primary carers
- child and any siblings in attendance
- parent(s) and education practitioners

Family Support

Relationships are nurtured between:

- child and close family members
- practitioners and family members including siblings, grandparents and others thought of as family

Intended primary outcomes

- Bonds of attachment between baby or infant and parent(s) or other primary care givers and then attachment to a growing number of other family members
- Effective helping relationships between practitioners and parents and then other close family members

Figure 3: Relationships in early child and family support

Relationships

The topics discussed in this section are:

- Relationships around a baby or infant who has very special needs
- Active listening
- Avoiding assumptions
- A balance of power
- Negotiating ways forward

Relationships around a baby or infant who has very special needs

Relationships lie at the heart of everything around babies and young children who have very special needs. They are the foundation of all work in health, education and family support. If we manage to get the relationships right, then a lot of good things can happen. But then this is true for almost all human activity.

At the beginning there is the attachment relationship between the new child and parent or parents and others with a parenting role. The baby comes equipped to attach as a matter of survival. When a parent or other adult responds, a bond is formed which can deepen with time and be long-lasting. Grandparents, siblings and other family adults can form bonds of attachment as they spend quality time with the growing baby or infant.

We know a great deal about attachment with infants who are developing typically. We know children do generally less well as they grow up when they did not have opportunities early in life to form bonds of attachment. Less is known about attachment issues with the children we are concerned with in this book. My logic tells me that in the matter of attachment, there can be no essential difference between children developing typically and those with very special needs in terms of need and benefit.

But there can be some features in children who have very special needs that can make attachment more of a challenge, for example when a vision impaired baby cannot return the mother's gaze. Also, some aspects of traditional support agencies in the countries I know about can get in the way and impede bonds of attachment – some professional activity, intended only to be helpful, is counterproductive. A common example of this is when too many appointments in too many places keep parent and child busy, anxious, tired and stressed. Surely, attachment requires calm and quiet times for child and parent to relax with each other, get to know each other and fall in love.

Then there are developing relationships between the family adults and the practitioners helping the child. Some practitioners will have a brief involvement while others might be helping the child over weeks, months or years. Professor Hilton Davis[11] has done a lot of work on the nature of these relationships between family adults and practitioners. He tells us that no practitioner can successfully help a disabled child with special needs in the long term without establishing what he terms a 'helping relationship' with the child's parent or parents.

The qualities practitioners require for helping relationship include respect, empathy, genuineness, humility, quiet enthusiasm and personal integrity. When parents and practitioners can relate to each other with honesty, respect and trust, the child and family has a much better chance of benefitting from whatever interventions are being offered. This is true even at the beginning of life when the warm relationships between parents and staff members in a NICU or SCBU can support and encourage parents to relate to their new child and begin bonding. In early child and family support, success is dependent on effective relationships in all three pillars – health, education and family support.

While some practitioners are by nature or experience better equipped for relationships of this sort, Davis' experience is that all of us will benefit from training. It must follow that parents also differ in their capacities for these relationships. We cannot assume that either group, parents or practitioners, are, by nature, more able to develop helping relationships.

---

[11] Davis, H. (2010) The Helping Relationship: Understanding Partnerships. *Interconnections Quarterly Journal,* **6,** p 23 and
Davis, H. & Day, C. (2010) *Working in Partnership: The Family Partnership Model.* London: Pearson

Darling, your physiotherapist is here

Agencies and their practitioners carry a responsibility to be aware of the importance of effective helping relationships and to become ever more competent in nurturing them. Parents and other family members do not carry a professional responsibility in this and are not likely to be offered training (though it can happen in some places). But all adult family members have life experience before this stage in their lives and most will have developed some insight into the potential for good relationships to achieve more than poor ones.

It is my experience that an essential element of these relationships is an ability and willingness to just be human. When a practitioner is in an effective helping relationship with a parent, on one level it is a therapist (for example) relating to a mother or father. On another level, it is one human being helping another human being at a time of need. The helping relationship has a much greater chance of success when the parent can see the real human being in the practitioner and the practitioner can see the real human being in each family member. Human kindness has a very important part to play in early child and family support.

It might come about that very many practitioners become involved, some with a close involvement, some seeing the child less often and some with an infrequent, but still necessary, involvement. If there is a flow of information in all directions between these practitioners and including the parents, then there is a network with, hopefully, the child and family at its centre. If all the relationships are as effective as they can be, then it will be a supportive network. If relationships are poor, everyone in the network can become very frustrated with benefits to the child and family reduced or negated. When being at the centre of a support network is overwhelming or difficult to manage for a parent, then a trusted practitioner might take on the role of keyworker and sit at the centre with them. This keyworker can aid the flow of accessible, jargon-free information, both to and from the family. This is an important part of the TAC approach.

Active listening

I see skilled listening as a valid therapeutic activity – a therapeutic activity that does not necessarily have to result in some sort of practical action and does not necessarily have to come from a therapist or counsellor. At one level, listening is a gift one human being can give to another. It can acknowledge the plight and feelings of the other and provide some release of built-up pressure. On a more skilled level, what Professor Davis terms 'active listening' can bring other benefits. These can include creating a safe space for people to sort out mental confusions and contradictions. Parents, grandparents and siblings of any age might have a bewildering mix of emotions. In my experience, these can be talked through allowing new insights and perhaps taking some power out of negative thoughts and feelings. This requires a trusting relationship and, probably, a sequence of conversations. Siblings, as children or teenagers, will benefit from the same approach but tailored to their level of maturity.

No practitioner should embark on this lightly. They must be strong enough to deal with whatever comes up. Any practitioner who meets parents with such fears as, *'I hope the mother does not want to talk about the child dying.'* or *'I will not cope if the father starts crying.'* is not ready to be an active listener. For their own sake and for the sake of the person they are trying to help, practitioners must know the limits of their competence. Agencies would do well to offer training and guidelines to support their practitioners in active listening. This can guide practitioners in knowing when to suggest a parent or other family member could see a counsellor, psychologist or other trained person.

Avoiding assumptions

Assumptions are not helpful. Acting on assumptions is a recipe for trouble. An example can be when parent and practitioner first meet each other. First impressions can lead to wrong assumptions. The parent or the practitioner might be nervous and ill at ease. The parent might have put on a smiling face to hide tiredness and worries and to give the impression of coping well. The practitioner might be deliberately jolly to hide anxiety about meeting the challenges this family brings. If the parent has already met a string of practitioners who have let the child and family down in some way, then there might not be much optimism in meeting another one. Practitioners who have worked with dozens of children might forget that this new child and family is entirely unique. First meetings can be a cause for anxiety. They will have the best chance of success when each person can decide to be a sensitive human being at that time and make the effort to listen properly without making assumptions. Each then is helping the other.

Other assumptions to avoid include those about race, culture, gender, relationship, competence and attitudes to disability. Here are some examples from my own work:

- I have supported many parents with intellectual disabilities who, contrary to the view of some practitioners around them, could make entirely rational decisions about the care of their child if they were properly supported in understanding the issues involved.

- A new mother of a baby with Down's Syndrome told me she was having a real struggle to reassess her long-held negative attitudes to and assumptions about disabled people in general. She felt she was succeeding in this struggle.
- Two young parents I knew were not upset to learn that their baby was blind because they were just grateful she was alive. Their doctor had been very apprehensive about breaking the news to them.
- A new mother who cried during all of the first sessions with me as keyworker was eventually able to articulate that she was not as upset about her baby daughter's disability as about not giving her young son a perfect little sister. This is a reminder that when someone is crying, we should not assume we know why.
- When parents of a baby I worked with came to the point of separation, there was surprise among all the child's practitioners when it was the mother who left home.

Practitioners must always be prepared for the unexpected. Avoiding assumptions is a professional requirement. Thoughtful anticipations are more constructive than assumptions. An experienced practitioner might meet a new parent with a mental check list (but not a clipboard!) of issues that could be explored sooner or later. This can include how much sleep the child and family are getting, how well the accommodation meets the family's current needs, if difficulties in family relationships are developing, how far stresses and strains are affecting child and parents' mental states, and so on. Such conversations will require unhurried time, a private space, empathy and active listening skills.

A balance of power

The child belongs to the parents (or those given a parental role) and the ultimate responsibility for children's upbringing and education lies with their parents. Though parents can seek advice and support from others, all decisions about the child are for the parents to make. This is generally true for parents of all children. The exceptions come when a court of law has to intervene for some reason.

Many practitioners will talk of working in partnership with parents. This is to be greatly welcomed as an antidote to those aloof practitioners in out-dated support agencies who tend to look down on parents, feeling it is their job to tell them what to do. But, for many reasons, this partnership cannot really be an equal one. One reason is that practitioners might carry authority to grant or deny an element of support, for example a financial benefit or a piece of equipment the child needs. Also, agencies and practitioners can label parents as 'good enough' or 'not good enough' with all the potential far-reaching consequences when the judgement is written down and available to others. Parents can also select or reject support from an agency or a practitioner and can make informal or formal complaints. They are not powerless.

Typically, in the countries I have experience of, agencies and their practitioners hold more power than parents. They set the arrangements for appointments and decide who needs to be present at meetings. Most encounters will be in the practitioners' premises where they are at ease and in control. Their language will be professional with a mix of jargon with which parents might not be familiar but nervous of saying so. It is very probable that the practitioners will have the advantage of college or university education giving them a perceived class, social or educational advantage or superiority over many of the parents they encounter.

I am not suggesting practitioners are power hungry or that parents are meek and ineffective. But the traditional medical mode can lead easily to a power imbalance in which practitioners take charge at the very time when new parents are low in confidence because of what they are going through. In these situations, parents are at a serious disadvantage in discussions about their child. They struggle, perhaps in vain, to be equal partners.

So power is an almost inevitable feature of practitioner-parent interactions. Acknowledging and managing a power imbalance becomes a necessary skill in building helping relationships. Practitioners might need to find ways to address this imbalance in their work *before* they talk of empowering parents. Part of an approach for practitioners to disempower themselves as far as possible, is to meet parents first as a human being before moving into skilled-practitioner mode. I have heard practitioners describing this as, *'Leaving the bag of tricks outside for the time being'*.

Negotiating ways forward

It would be counterproductive for parents and their practitioners to be continually in conflict with each other and unable to agree on decisions about the child. This happens rarely in my experience. Skills in negotiating can be helpful in resolving difficult issues and in building and maintaining helping relationships. At the most basic level, negotiations can be just good manners, for instance when a practitioner on a home visit asks, *'Where would you like me to sit?'*, *'Do you mind if I make a few notes?'* Such considerations help the practitioner avoid appearing overbearing and disempowering parents in their own home.

A deeper level of negotiating skills is required in some issues, for example about the idea of the child starting in a mother & baby group, playgroup or nursery. Such a step might seem natural and routine for a practitioner but a very big step for some parents. If the parent strongly feels they and/or the child are not ready, then this decision must be respected. There will be other opportunities to discuss it again in time. When a parent is not keen on the idea but is open for discussion with the practitioner, both can air their points of view and perhaps clear up any misunderstandings or wrong assumptions either one is holding. Perhaps some practical precautions can be discussed when a parent has valid misgivings about how well the new group or centre will cater for the child's unique and very special health and care needs. The discussion might result in an agreement to take the big step now or to wait awhile and then consider again.

There can be more difficult negotiations when parents and practitioners disagree about a treatment, therapy or educational programme. Skilled negotiation can resolve the issue only when neither party is determined to have everything their own way. Entering a negotiation means being willing to move to some extent. Both sides must be willing to listen and to try to understand the other's point of view. Perhaps a workable compromise can be agreed on the shared basis of having the child's wellbeing at heart. Perhaps a neutral person more skilled in negotiating can be brought in as a mediator. Failure in negotiation can lead to appeals to courts of law when the decision is taken out of the hands of both parents and practitioners.

I am making no assumptions here that either practitioners or parents are automatically more skilled in negotiation. In my work I have seen examples of both. But, if negotiation is an integral part of supporting families of children who have very special needs, then some training ought to be available to practitioners and parents.

Lastly, I argue that practitioners should never offer advice of the, 'What I would do if I were you is…' sort. This interference is neither helpful nor respectful. But a parent or other family member might approach a practitioner with some dilemma they are facing. The respectful response is for the practitioner to help gather all relevant information about the issue, for instance the pros and cons of some additional treatment or therapy, and then, if required, discuss it all with them. What the family member then decides to do is a matter for them, but at least now perhaps they can make a more informed and considered decision.

Negative mental states shared by parents and practitioners

There are many negative mental states practitioners can suffer in common with parents and other family members. Examples are denial, hope, worry and guilt. We are all subject to these mental states from time to time. When they become problematic, there can be help from family, friends, managers, psychologists, psychiatrists, spiritual leaders and others. I am writing here from my direct experience as a teacher and family keyworker, not as a professional trained in these subjects.

It is quite common for an insensitive practitioner to describe a parent they know as being in denial. Blame is attached. There can be a subtext, 'It is *about time they pulled themselves together'*. In my experience, denial is a common coping mechanism for all of us. When a new baby has a disabling condition, one parent might accept the news while a partner at first refuses to listen to the evidence. A grandparent might deny the situation and say to one of the parents, *'You were just like that as a baby, but you grew out of it'*. Being in denial can be a coping mechanism to help us get through a bad time. It is a short-term strategy.

A parent or practitioner who stays in denial for a long time might need help. A parent who, in denial of their young child's disability, persists in refusing to use a wheelchair or another piece of equipment that would benefit the child is doing a disservice to the child. Any observation by a practitioner that a parent is stuck in denial must be followed by an offer of professional help to the parent. This is more constructive than criticism and blame. A practitioner whose habitual behaviour pattern with parents is to be brusque and insensitive might be trying to avoid acknowledging children's pain or parents' distress. This practitioner is not coping and needs support. It can be that some practitioners will want to maintain their narrow discipline-specific focus on a child's condition rather than face the implications of the whole multifaceted condition.[12] Denial is common in both practitioners and family members.

Then there is hope, worry and guilt. These states of mind will surely be familiar to parents of all children and to practitioners and managers. They seem to come as part of the human condition but can become stronger in people around children who have very special needs.

Hope and worry first. Both take us away from the task in hand, away from where we are now to where we might be in the future. I think of hope as daydreaming about what we do want in the future and worry as day-dreaming about what we do not want in the future. Both are natural: it seems we all have hopes and we all have worries. Many practitioners assert

---

[12] Bartram, P. (2009) The Eye of the Sea - A response to the article, TAC for the 21st century: A unifying theory about children who have multifaceted disabilities. *Interconnections Quarterly Journal,* **7,** p 6

that we should never try to take anyone's hope away. So, when a parent says they hope their child will one day walk or talk or hold down a job or get married, the sensitive practitioner acknowledges the hope and then outlines the first essential steps on any of these long roads. I think this can be so whether or not the practitioner expects the child to get very far along the particular road. But, in my view, it is a wise approach because it marries hope to constructive action, perhaps with hope providing a first motivation for the effort needed.

We probably cannot take hope away even if we wanted to, but we should try to help when someone seems lost in hope and hardly able to be in the present moment doing what needs to be done. Much of this applies to worry. Perhaps, like hope, it has a spectrum with two extremes. At one end, there is some worry or anxiety that spurs a person into action – going back to turn the gas off, seeking advice when a rash is not going away. At the other end are states of worry and anxiety that take over, sapping our spirit and energy and leaving us inert on the sofa. The mind is absorbed in an imagined unpleasant future and unable to do very much about what needs doing now. When practitioners see parents lost much of the time in worry towards this end of the spectrum, they need guidance from their agency about what to do.

Persistent negative states of mind might tip over into longer-term mental ill health. At some point, parents lost in these mental states must be asked if they would like to talk to a qualified person. Agency managers must also watch out for practitioners who are getting bogged down in these mental states and becoming less able to perform in the here and now.

Guilt can be a very big issue. It seems to come in the same human package as caring, kindness and responsibility and parents of all children can be subject to it from time to time. Perhaps guilt emerges each time we feel we are not caring as much as we should. Some parents of the children we are talking about in this book are particularly vulnerable to guilt because of the elevated level of care that is needed. This might be with nutrition, excretion, respiration and medication to help the child stay healthy and survive. The child might require constant attention day and night to reduce discomfort, pain, crying or anxiety. Then there is the conscious and careful effort to help the child acquire new understanding and skills. The natural parental response of love and care for a typically developing child can be magnified many times when a baby or young child has very special needs with the result that a mother or father can feel they can never do enough. Feelings of guilt can emerge at any time of the day or night.

If guilt stays locked in a parent's mind, it can assume crippling proportions and leave no room for pleasure, joy, satisfaction or self-esteem. This will impact on all family relationships and detract from the energy, optimism and positive attitude that bringing up children requires. Parents for whom feelings of guilt have become a troubling issue would do well to find someone to talk to. A skilled listener will offer first help and, if necessary, suggest further steps to help the situation. Managers, supervisors and students' tutors must be watchful for this level of guilt in practitioners and students who have perhaps realised their limitations, realised with a jolt that they do not have a magic wand to make everything better.

It is essential for practitioners and parents to know that there are no magic wands – at least, not in my experience. The needs and situations of some of these babies and young children we are talking about and of their families are complex, fraught, subject to difficult decisions and evoke strong emotions. It is unlikely they will be resolved by any sort of quick fix. When parents know this, it can help them avoid investing too much hope in each agency and practitioner they meet and then being disappointed, frustrated and angry.

When practitioners know they do not carry a magic wand, they can keep their work with a child and family in perspective, being aware that they are inevitably limited in what they can achieve. Professional concern and commitment varies greatly. A practitioner who is content to offer minimum effort will not be welcomed by any family and might be discounted. A practitioner who desperately wants to do everything and then more will go home at the end of each day feeling despondent and might lie awake worrying about the things they have not done. This brings the danger of burning out – then not being able to help any families.

In summary, we each carry some responsibility for our own mental or psychological wellbeing and for the psychological wellbeing of the people close to us. This is part of our humanity and an important issue for everyone involved with children who have very special needs. I suggest the following as a guide:

- Parents and other family adults should talk to one of their practitioners if they feel some negative mental state is overwhelming them.
- Siblings of babies and infants who have very special needs might also have a bewildering mix of emotions and need skilled help.
- Practitioners who are concerned about a parent's mental state should know when and how to approach them to offer support.
- Managers and practitioners who are concerned about a colleague's mental state should know when and how to approach them to offer support.

The support needed for parents, siblings or practitioners might need to be from a qualified person in the relevant field.

Becoming an advocate or champion

In the world of disability there are strong elements for children and adults of prejudice, discrimination, unfair treatment and unmet needs. This can be the backdrop against which family members and practitioners work with care, concern and commitment. In this situation, parents and practitioners can find themselves becoming advocates or champions.

By 'advocate' I mean one person who takes on another's cause to try to improve their situation. Many parents speak of becoming fighters, first entering battles for effective support for their new child, then for appropriate schooling, then for transition into suitable adult provision. This is not a role they would have chosen. Many parents have told me they were previously calm and amenable people and now find themselves in fighting mode much of the time. Siblings and grandparents can become advocates too. There is a trap here that many parents and other family members cannot help falling into: advocacy is demanding work that drains time, energy and spirit and yet adults around children who have very special needs feel they are given no choice.

Many practitioners, sooner or later, will find themselves stepping out of their usual role to argue with their own agency or another agency, for better support for a particular child on their case list. There is another of my spectrums here, from easy-going practitioners at one end to practitioners at the other extreme who take a pro-child stance and will not let go. Doggedness and professional seniority help in this but there is always the danger of falling foul of the employing agency.

In my working life I have met many parents and practitioners becoming advocates to the great cost to their own health and wellbeing. This sort of advocacy might start with a very worrying dilemma – to speak up or keep quiet. I greatly admire people who speak up. Often, a battle won for one child will benefit others.

The Vietnamese Buddhist monk, Thich Nhat Hanh[13] offers wise words about this dilemma about speaking up that every practitioner will face from time to time:

> *'The voice of caring and understanding must be distinct
> from the voice of ambition.'*

By 'champion' I mean someone advocating for a group or people to get improved support from a local authority or a national government. In many cases, family members join with other parents and, perhaps, practitioners to launch a campaign or set up a new organisation to raise awareness and bring about change. This can be a local, national or international effort. Many of the established charities in the UK were started in this way. Sadly, with time, the initial passion and drive can be lost with the charity falling victim to inflexible bureaucracy, institutionalism and government control.

---

[13] Hanh, T. N. (1987) *Interbeing: Commentaries on the Tiep Hien Precepts.* Berkeley: Parallax Press p 50

People who set up new charities can face a dilemma about how to run their new organisation. Staying small can help preserve the original philosophy, principles and good practice. Growing into an ever larger organisation will mean that more people can be helped but some principles and good practice can be lost as a consequence. Buying or renting property for offices and paying attractive salaries to chief executives and managers can divert funds from the original purpose. Charities that choose this option can soon find they resemble large companies with powerful people at the top of a vertical hierarchy and vulnerable people at the bottom[14]. Paid staff members might well enjoy a quality of life the people who need to use the charity will never have. Inevitably, chief executives will soon have to put up with advocates and champions banging on their doors![15]

---

[14] Limbrick, P. (2012) *Horizontal Teamwork in a Vertical World: Exploring interagency collaboration and people empowerment.* Clifford: Interconnections

[15] For a wider discussion of society's responsibility to vulnerable children and adults: Limbrick, P. (2016) *Caring Activism: A 21st century concept of care.* Clifford: Interconnections

7

Unhelpful features of out-dated support

Traditional agencies and the practitioners in them, following approaches common in the last century, can do some things which are unhelpful and omit to do other things that might have helped. Babies and infants who have very special needs and their families can be adversely affected by ill-thought-out patterns of support or left with very significant unmet needs – all impacting on the child's wellbeing and learning and on the family's quality of live and perhaps survival.

I describe some aspects of out-dated support as insensitive, harsh or institutional. I am using the word institutional to characterise provision that is impersonal, inflexible, meeting the needs of agencies rather than of children and families, neglectful of human rights, and persisting only because it is the cheapest and easiest option. My description of out-dated support is meant as a comment on how some agencies model their support systems and is not meant to characterise the practitioners working in those systems. I have met very many genuine, sensitive and empathetic practitioners in both traditional and modern agencies.

I am describing unhelpful approaches under three headings as follows:

- Confusion about parent and practitioner roles
- Fragmented support
- Unnatural support

Confusion about parent and practitioner roles

In this section on confusion of roles, I will address three questions:

- Whose child is it?
- Whose needs are being met?
- Can new parents know what they want?

Whose child is it?

It is not an inappropriate question. Parents often report that practitioners move in on them, sensitively or insensitively, when the baby or infant has very special needs in a way they would not do with other parents. Parents of typically developing infants are left largely to their own devices with freedom to use their natural parenting skills and learn as they go along. If parents stay within the very broad limits set by their culture and society, they are not checked or taught or challenged.

Parents might lose this freedom when their baby or infant has very special needs. From the first hours or days of the child's life, there can be an expanding host of experts telling parents what to do and how to do it. The

assumption is that practitioners know best and that new parents know little or nothing. There is an unspoken message to parents that bringing up the child must now be a group effort led by experts.

Few parents at this time can resist this takeover and will take to heart the message that they are not up to the task of bringing up their new child. The result can then be a very dangerous mix of an infant with very special needs and parent or parents who are undermined, deskilled and feeling out of control. In out-of-date support, agencies and their practitioners put themselves in charge of the child's development and learning, taking confidence and autonomy from parents. In a modern approach parents' rights and responsibility to bring up their children are acknowledged with practitioners respecting and supporting parents' natural parenting skills while remaining acutely aware of the dangers of appearing to be powerful.

An expert approach can be appropriate, for instance when doctors and nurses are investigating illness and prescribing treatment. This is a valued expertise, but it loses its relevance when supporting families in the long term with their child's learning. Practitioners supporting babies and young children who have very special needs cannot stand aloof as experts offering tried and tested solutions. They must work flexibly in relationship and partnership bringing respect, sensitivity and humility into their work. Ideally, for babies and infants this can be a three-way partnership involving infant, parent and practitioner learning from each other.

Many parents, for valid reasons, first make themselves subsidiary to experts and then, seeing the limitations, try to reclaim their status as autonomous parents and lead partners in their child's care.

Whose needs are being met?

We might all assume early childhood intervention agencies are designed to meet the needs of children and families. Perhaps this is how they all began. But something happens in traditional services that turns it all around so that parents come to feel the needs of the agency and of the people working in it are the priority. It can appear the practitioners are important while the children and parents are not. It can be that families get locked into an inflexible process which can appear, at worst, as a conveyor belt onto which babies and infants drop.

In my working experience, multidisciplinary assessment events can be an example of this. Here is the experience of Adam's family:

> Adam's parents reported to the keyworker that there had been some sort of assessment day when he was about ten months old. This was in a local child development centre separate from the hospital. They had tried to put it out of their minds because it had been so unpleasant and could not remember who had been present. Adam had reacted negatively to each person, cried, screamed and then slept. The discussion at the end was full of negatives. Both parents left the centre feeling extremely angry. The day had achieved nothing as far as they were concerned; they had been patronised and unfair judgements had been made about Adam based on activities in which he was unsettled, unhappy and afraid. If a report of the day had been sent to them, they had not kept it. When interventionists did begin work with the child some time later they were not the same ones they had met at the assessment as far as the parents could remember.[16]

There might be a medical need for a meeting to agree a diagnosis of the child's condition, give it a name if possible and prescribe treatments. This is different from the educational need to learn about the child and decide how to promote new understanding and skills. In traditional support, these two needs have been inappropriately put together as 'The Assessment'.

In early child and family support learning about a child's abilities and needs can happen naturally and unobtrusively in the TAC process[17]. Here, observing and teaching go hand in hand. Parents are listened to and are in control. Infants are involved in their natural activity. As practitioners get involved in the real life of the child and family, observations and activities to help the child acquire new understanding and skills fall into place naturally.

---

[16] *Primary Interventionists in the Team Around the Child Approach* p 38

[17] Limbrick, P. (2003) *An Integrated Pathway for Assessment and Support: For children with complex needs and their families.* UK: Interconnections

If there is a need for some sort of medical assessment event, it can be carefully designed to be respectful of and sensitive to the needs of child and parent, timed to fit around the child's times for feeding and sleeping, and with an intent to answer both practitioners' and parents' questions.

Can new parents know what they want?

There is often a wrong assumption in my experience that they cannot. This can lead to well-meaning practitioners taking charge in expert mode. It is true, unsurprisingly, that new parents will not know, for example, what sort of physiotherapy their baby needs or how to compensate for impaired vision. But they will know they want some sort of emotional support. They will know they want help to understand what is going on. They will know they need help in learning how to look after their baby. When a sensitive practitioner has time to listen, all of this will become apparent.

It is unreasonable to expect that new parents will ask the questions practitioners think they should be asking and then blame them for being naïve when they do not. With support, parents will soon ask other questions as they learn about their new child and as they listen to practitioners who know so much more than they do at the beginning.

Fragmented support

Fragmented support for babies and infants who have very special needs and a multifaceted condition and their families is unhelpful in three ways:

- Treating children as though they come in bits
- A disorganised pattern of support
- Overloading child and family

Treating children as though they come in bits

I have already touched on the persistent professional myth that, when supporting a young child's understanding and skills, we can address each facet of a child's functioning separately from the others – as though they were not interconnected and interdependent facets of a whole child. Very few parents would fall into this trap. They treat young children as whole beings. This is part of natural parenting and we can learn a lot from it.

Discipline-specific interventions for these new children come from medical thinking. Trying to apply them to a baby or infant's learning shows us how far the medical tradition has led some agencies and practitioners down the wrong path. Progress towards effective support means practitioners improving their skills in seeing the whole child and contributing to collective competence. Each practitioner must be able to switch as necessary between:

- focusing on part of a child's functioning
- working with the whole child in relevant activities that integrate all aspects of the child's functioning

The out-of-date fragmented discipline-specific approach meets the needs of practitioners more than that of children and families. The approach is entirely unnatural and prevents babies, infants and parents joining abilities together into meaningful whole-child activity.

A disorganised pattern of support

When multiple practitioners are involved with a baby or infant, there can be disorganisation, confusion and chaos. Disorganisation can create two problems; practitioners do not know what each other is doing and a chaotic routine of appointments wastes everyone's time and energy.

When the people supporting the emergence of new understanding and skills in the young child do not share their observations and approaches with each other, they have to work 'blind'. A practitioner supporting posture and movement cannot know or use the communication approach another practitioner has designed for the child. A practitioner helping the child make the best use of hearing and vision skills has to work in ignorance of the child's posture requirements. It might also be that none of these prac-titioners have taken time to learn what the parents have already discovered about their child. When there are no opportunities to share information, practitioners, parents and children work at a disadvantage. Fragmented support means practitioners cannot support each other's work to give the child increased opportunities to practice new understanding and skills. Separate programmes cannot be integrated into the child's play, socialising, mealtimes, management of clothes, etc.

Multiple appointments can involve child and parent in frequent journeys that are time-consuming, difficult and expensive – more so when there are young siblings. There might be no consideration of the infant's feeding and sleeping times and no thought given to how many other appointments there are on the same day or in the same week in other places. When practitioners act independently of each other or even in ignorance of who else is involved, all opportunities for creating a manageable timetable of appointments are lost. The result of this institutional approach is more exhaustion, frustration and stress for child and family and a drain on family finances.

In fragmented support of this sort, the preferred working patterns of agencies and their practitioners take precedence over the family's need for a well-organised manageable pattern of appointments and for coherent whole-child interventions.

Overloading child and family

When support is fragmented, there cannot be regular consideration of whether there are too many or too few people involved in the child's learning. There is no way of knowing if some specific professional expertise is lacking or if the child and family are sinking under the weight of too many agencies and practitioners. And then collective remedies are not possible.

Overloading and confusion can come from the traditional additive approach that provides a separate practitioner for each of the child's diagnoses or suspected diagnoses. The antidote to this lies in the ingenuity of the people in the child's TAC. Once there is a whole picture of the child and family's needs and of the problems arising from the way support is provided, solutions will become evident.

In the wealthy countries I have experience of, there can be too many practitioners involved in a baby or infant's development and learning when the child has a multifaceted condition. Strangely, while parents would like fewer practitioners involved, their practitioners might each be overwhelmed by the number of children on their case list! On the other hand, some children and families in some parts of the world must make do as best they can in the absence of particular practitioners. This situation is discussed with great imagination and ingenuity in 'Disabled Village Children'[18]. I feel the spirit of this book has relevance for families in all countries.

Unnatural support

In the UK and some countries I know of, when a baby or young child has a multifaceted condition, the child, parents and other family members can get sucked into outdated processes that have no thought for their human rights or quality of life. These processes often have a strong medical flavour and are inappropriately modelled on procedures for curing a patient of any age who has some sort of short-term illness. In these institutional approaches, children are invalidated or downgraded by having very special needs. They can be thought inferior and not deserving of very much.

This might seem like a very strong indictment of society, its attitudes and the support it provides. However, we find the same prejudiced attitudes at play when older disabled children are thought not deserving of good education or normal social activity and when disabled adults are denied employment, decent housing, marriage opportunities and a decent sex life. We only have to take our minds back a few decades to find babies, children, teenagers and adults incarcerated in institutions for their whole lives. Often on medical advice, children were given up by their parents and abandoned to a miserable and abusive existence out of public view.

Reform came in the UK in the 1980s when many of these institutions were closed down. But as I write there are repeated stories in the press about children who have special needs ending up in secure hospital provision

---

[18] Werner, D. (1987) *Disabled Village Children: A guide for community health workers, rehabilitation workers, and families.* Berkeley: Hesperian

where they suffer abusive treatment – sometimes in solitary confinement.[19] In my view, the root cause of this social injustice is prejudice and discrimination – a pervasive attitude that people, young and old, who have disabilities and special needs are not deserving of human rights. We see the same pervasive prejudiced and discriminatory attitudes towards black people, first nations, women and others.

As long as these attitudes persist, there will be unnatural, disrespectful, inhuman and institutional treatment of children and adults who have very special needs. This includes attitudes to parents of disabled children who frequently report being treated as though they themselves had an intellectual disability. In traditional support in the pre-school years, children and families can find themselves up against this social prejudice integrated into medical approaches that still have a strong institutional flavour.

In my view, we can see outdated support for babies and infants who have very special needs and their families and the prevalent attitudes within traditional agencies as a halfway point between institutional care and a sensitive respectful approach that fully recognising the rights of children and parents. My reasons for this strong view include the following:

- Parents are suddenly involved with agencies in processes they have not actively opted for over which they have no control.
- Parents and other adult family members can find themselves patronised, criticised and disempowered at a time when they are in crisis and needing sensitive support.
- Babies and infants can be subject to medical procedures that take little account of pain or levels of anxiety.

---

[19] For one recent story visit: http://www.tacinterconnections.com/index.php/allnews/developmentsintreatment/3025-a-teen-with-autism-is-locked-in-solitary-confinement-and-being-fed-through-a-hatch-have-we-really-moved-on-from-bedlam-uk and
http://www.tacinterconnections.com/index.php/allnews/productsservices/3070-joint-committee-on-human-rights-jchr-detention-of-children-and-young-people-with-learning-disabilities-and-or-autism-inquiry-uk

- When interventions are planned, there might be no thought given to child-parent bonds of attachment.
- Parent and child might have to travel to a variety of places for treatment sessions. While in some cases this might be unavoidable, in other cases it is to meet agencies' needs with no thought given to the family's time pressures and tiredness.
- Attending appointments can be a drain on family finances because of travel, parking, eating out and child care.
- Appointments for these treatment sessions might not give any thought to the child's comfort, quality of life or to their routines for feeding, sleeping and playing.
- Babies and infants can be parked on waiting lists so that 'early' intervention comes later and later.
- Practitioners give themselves importance they do not give to parents. While they want their own understanding and skills to be respected, they do not respect what parents know and do.
- New parents find themselves having to share their parenting role with practitioners in partnerships – as inferior partners.
- Support for babies and infants' education can be offered primarily in clinical treatment sessions though the actual need is for a combined medical, educational and play approach.
- Babies and infants' need for natural learning in everyday activities is given secondary importance to goals set by practitioners in their clinical environments.
- Parents can be asked to continue therapy at home in conditions that are not ideal and with the spoken or unspoken threat that not to do so will disadvantage the child.

I am not suggesting any agency or practitioner wants to be cruel to children or parents, but there can be a prevalent medical/institutional hangover that we need to become aware of and address. When we see babies and young children who have very special needs as children with rights, we can ask ourselves if what we are doing is fair, respectful and appropriate. With this mindset we can explore how our interventions impact on parents, siblings, grandparents and other close family members. We can use rights and naturalness as essential measures of our work.

We can ask ourselves if the whole pattern of appointments at home and in clinics, centres and other places is endangering the calm and peaceful times the new child and parents need to form close bonds of attachment with each other. We can include proper consideration of attachment when children's needs are assessed and interventions planned.

Life with a baby or infant who has very special needs can be fulfilling and joyful. It can also be demanding and stressful with much to worry about, many questions to find answers to and so much to be done each day. There might be tensions in relationships as parents, siblings and grandparents adjust to this new unplanned situation. Local agencies and their practitioners must explore whether the whole pattern of interventions is helping the family situation or making it even worse.

In consideration of the young child's quality of life, we can explore to what extent the child has quality time at home learning naturally in everyday activities or having to endure frequent journeys away from home for treatment. Are there too many non-family adults expecting the baby or infant to accept being handled by them? Also, are outdated interventions robbing parents of their natural parenting skills and self esteem? Are siblings suffering from reduced attention as parents are kept too busy with appointments and home programmes?

*

Family life provides a natural safe space with a quality of life in which children are provided with the things they need and are given attention and respect. It is a matter of degree: no family is perfect, no children have a perfect childhood and in a minority of cases, family life breaks down. But family life is in the natural order of things in this world and ought to be the obvious starting point when thinking how to support new children who have very special needs.

It is my experience that as education and family support – two of the three essential pillars of early child and family support, take a bigger part in support for babies and infants who have very special needs, so such human qualities as naturalness and respect come to the fore. While I have met very many sensitive and admirable health practitioners, I see an urgent need for reform of the services they are part of to eradicate medical/institutional traditions that are neither child nor parent-centred.

8

Concluding remarks

My purpose in this book has been to contrast the old with the new in support for babies and infants who have very special needs and their families. The time span for this is, more or less, my own lifetime and this coincides with the existence in the UK of the national health service (NHS). I have described an effective early child and family support system and contrasted it with out-of-date traditional approaches. I have contrasted support that is mostly in the medical mode with support that brings together the three modes of health, education and family support. I have labelled the worst of out-of-date practices as insensitive and institutional. All the elements of the effective early child and family support I have described are in use in one country or another but are rarely found together as a complete system.

When we are thinking of moving towards 21st century support for babies and young children who have very special needs and their families, it can be helpful to acknowledge where we are now – what we are trying to move away from. I have described unhelpful features of outdated support without going into detail about infants being treated with unthinking cruelty and parents being humiliated and reduced to tears. But then nor have I talked about those practitioners whom some parents think of as angels who go out of their way to treat children and families with kindness and respect.

These contrasts have persisted in early childhood intervention since the middle of last century. Perhaps we should not be surprised because recent history of how we treat children (in my country and perhaps in yours) has stories of both horror and of genuine caring – and, somewhere between the two, a crude sentimentality that does no one any good.

Knowing the 20th century history of institutional incarceration in the UK, I am not surprised if this disregard for the rights, wellbeing and proper care of children with disabilities persists in some agencies – not surprised if there are still some institutional attitudes in the medical world. Then there are the still prevalent prejudiced attitudes to people of all ages who are disabled and particularly to those with a learning or intellectual disability. In the face of this denial of rights and quality of life for disabled adults and schoolchildren, why should we be surprised if it impacts on babies and young children?

We are not starting from an enlightened position and change is never easy to achieve. On the positive side, there are very many examples in early childhood intervention of consideration and compassion. We must build on these.

This book is written for parents, students and practitioners and none of these people are powerless. We have a strong tradition in the UK of parents getting together and bringing about change, both locally and nationally. Unfortunately, we do not have a strong tradition of agencies approaching parents with a genuine desire to find out what they feel about the support they are getting. Too often, support is provided on assumptions with more regard for what practitioners want to do than what families need.

Practitioners can influence their agencies. In my view this is a professional responsibility, but it depends on practitioners not being stuck in out-of-date attitudes. Students can assess their course content in the light of rights and discrimination, naturalness and institutionalism, modernity and tradition, kindness and insensitivity and then struggle for change, if necessary, when they are established in work.

I have written about creating change in other books, but my main message for now is that parents who want to become powerful must join other like-minded parents. Similarly, practitioners who want to bring about change must join up with other like-minded practitioners. Then, in the spirit of partnership, those parents and practitioners must join together. The spirit of a compassionate society is for people to become powerful *with* others rather than powerful *over* others (the situation we must escape from).

Agencies can begin the process of change by consulting local families. Parents will be willing, first by helping frame the consultation, then by discussing issues, then by helping plan and enact change. Once it is acknowledged that children belong to their parents, it is a logical step to acknowledge that agencies belong more to families (who pay for them with their taxes) than to professionals. Again, the way forward is in genuine partnership. Using this book and others, parents and/or practitioners can write a charter for change.

*

In support of people around babies and infants who have very special needs, an international group has produced a free Guide entitled *'Are you worried about your child?'*[20] This was published online in 2018 for all to use and has since been translated into several languages. Anne Emerson, Associate Professor in Special Needs Education, University of Nottingham, UK is one of the authors. She has written the following to introduce the guide:

> *When a baby is identified as having disabilities or complex and long-term health conditions their parents experience a range of distressing emotions which can include trauma. They may be told that their child will not achieve any independent skills or even that their child's life is in danger. However empathic the health professionals are who deliver this news it still comes as a shock and can be catastrophic.*
>
> *From this point family life is over-turned, it impacts on the close and extended family, often breaking natural support systems. Parents can feel*

---

[20] Boucher, S et al. (2018) *'Are you worried about your child?'* A guide to support families of children with complex needs and the professionals who care for them
In English: http://www.tacinterconnections.com/images/Guide2-to-Support-Families-of-Children-with-Complex-Needs.pdf
Other languages: http://www.tacinterconnections.com/index.php/new-world-guide

helpless and hopeless which may impact on the bond between themselves and their baby. Most of all they often feel isolated, particularly when they do not know of anyone else who is in the same situation.

Research has shown that services are generally poor in meeting the needs of these families despite the numbers of health professionals who can be involved. Families report the need to manage multiple appointments and relationships with professionals. Ironically, some families find the professionals who are there to support their child inadvertently make life harder for parents and families.

An international group has written a guide in the form of letters to parents and professionals to introduce key experiences faced by many families in this situation and to highlight their needs. It is intended to help professionals think through the issues the families may face, and to develop a holistic view to the family needs. The specific need for systemic change to offer keyworkers and to utilise the Team Around the Child approach is highlighted.

Appendix 1: Occupational Therapists in Early Intervention

By Annemarie Sims

Occupational Therapists (OTs) are often found working in early childhood intervention. OTs are well suited to provide a 'naturalistic approach' as described in this book. OTs are trained to assess the barriers to a person's participation in everyday activities. These include tasks of their choosing and those that are essential to live a healthy life. These tasks are divided into self-care, productivity and leisure.

OTs recognise that a balance between all three areas is important to achieve optimal physical and mental health. The Canadian Model of Occupational Performance and Engagement developed by Polatajko, Townsend and Craik in 2007 illustrates the interplay between the person, the task and the environment and how this impacts the performance of the chosen activity (the occupation). The addition of the word *engagement* emphasises the importance of active participation of the individual.

This model can be applied to infants and young children with complex needs and their families. The OT's focus is maximising the infant's participation in everyday life as a member of their family. Intervention therefore focuses on what the parents identify as being the most important activities to optimise the quality of life for the child and the family. This is a 'task-oriented approach' whereby the task or occupation is the focus rather than the individual performance components within the child. For example an infant with increased muscle tone in their legs may present as a challenge for the caregiver to change their nappy. Instead of giving the parent separate exercises for the legs, the OT would demonstrate how to increase hip rotation and prevent contractures while changing the nappy, and how to position the infant to facilitate this important care giving task.

Another parent may feel strongly that their child needs to be able to self-feed. Then the OT would look at the barrier to feeding and work on that particular task rather than un-related fine motor activities. Play is often called the occupation of childhood. Here, OTs would focus on helping the young child access play rather than measuring specific motor skills. Therapy therefore happens as part of everyday activities in the child's natural environment and not as a separate and additional care giving chore.

Reference:

Polatajko, H. J., Townsend, E. A. & Craik, J. (2007). The Canadian Model of Occupational Performance and Engagement (CMOP-E). In E. A. Townsend & H. J. Polatajko (eds.), *Enabling Occupation II: Advancing an Occupational Therapy Vision of Health, Well-being, & Justice through Occupation*, Ottawa, ON: CAOT Publications ACE. 22-36.

*

Annemarie Sims is an Occupational Therapist who has been working with children for over 20 years. She has a special interest in neurodevelopmental disorders and infant and early childhood development.

Appendix 2: Questions a parent might need answers to

The list below illustrates how diverse early intervention needs might be and is offered to show that, frequently, there can be a mismatch between what a particular practitioner can offer and what a family are needing at that time.

Speaking from my own experience as a keyworker with the One Hundred Hours organisation in the 1990s, parents, during all of the early years, might be seeking any combination of the following elements of support when they encounter a new practitioner or a new service. (For an account of One Hundred Hours see Limbrick-Spencer, G. 2001.)

- To find out what is wrong with the child.
- To find out why this happened.
- To find out if there is a cure or a medical treatment.
- To find out the implications for any siblings.
- To find out if it is safe to have more children.
- To find out what the diagnosis means for the child's health, survival, wellbeing, happiness, education, adult life.
- To acquire an understanding of the condition.
- To find out what can be done to help the child.
- To find out what services and support are available.
- To acquire necessary skills to help in the child's treatment, care, play, development and learning.
- To get practical help from practitioners in the child's treatment, care, play, development and learning.
- To find words to use to explain the condition to strangers, neighbours, friends and relatives.
- To get support in helping partner, grandparents, siblings and friends understand the condition.
- To get support in encouraging and facilitating partner, relatives and friends to offer practical help.
- To get help in balancing the needs of the child with the needs of partner and siblings.
- To get support in maintaining the relationship with the partner.

- To get relevant services so that employment can be continued.
- To get help in remedying an immediate problem or cause of stress such as disturbed nights, the child's feeding, the child's constant crying or other challenging behaviour.
- To get such support as 'baby-sitting', childcare or short breaks to help in coping with stressful and difficult situations.
- To have someone to discuss issues with and to help parents come to informed decisions.
- To have someone to be a listening ear and a shoulder to cry on.
- To have counselling to help sort out emotions and to develop coping strategies.
- Help with getting benefits, applying for Family Fund[21] and other grants, securing money for items of equipment, managing the family budget.
- To get more appropriate housing by moving house, getting adaptations, equipment, etc.
- To get practical help with household tasks.
- To get opportunities for family members to spend valuable time apart from each other on rewarding activity – as happens naturally in most families.
- To get help in taking the child to such local facilities as mother and toddler groups, playgroups, nurseries, swimming pool, football matches, etc.
- To get help in keeping family life as normal as possible in relation to outings, socialising, leisure activities, holidays, etc.
- To be helped to make informed choices about the shape of the whole package of support so that it is a coherent whole which does not make family life impossible and which enhances aspirations of all family members.
- To have an adviser and advocate to help remove barriers to the parent's aspirations.

---

[21] Family Fund: https://www.familyfund.org.uk/

The list is long and wide-ranging because the challenges in caring for a child with sensory and multiple needs can affect every aspect of family life: finances, housing, leisure, employment, relationships, emotions, beliefs, etc. A parent who has all or many of the needs listed above and who might or might not have articulated them into clear ideas and wishes, can easily become frustrated when services and practitioners are found to have a narrow remit and when no services are found which are designed to meet particular needs.

Many practitioners who perceive needs which are beyond their own job description will do as much as they can to help. This might mean they put extra hours in and it might mean they have to distort the records they submit to their managers about how they have spent their time with clients. Such practitioners are often described by parents as saints and life-savers. This sort of under-the-counter support can help keep desperate parents going and help vulnerable families stay together.

*

[The text in this appendix is extracted from Birmingham University's School of Education Distance Learning Module: *Early Years Sensory and Multiple Needs: The Child in the Family, Unit 3: Evaluating the Work of Services*, written by Peter Limbrick and edited by Linda Watson.]

Appendix 3: How programmes can be integrated

An integrated intervention system requires that the main practitioners involved with the infant's development and learning integrate as appropriate their approaches and goals instead of working separately from each other. The infant's TAC meetings are the ideal forum for planning this and offer graded opportunities for this integration. The degree of integration is always a TAC decision – not forgetting that parents are full members. Stages of increasing integration are as follows:

Stage 1:

Practitioners and parents tell each other what they are working on with the child. This brings the benefit of seeing the pattern of interventions as a whole, resolving contradictory approaches and avoiding wasted time and effort when two people are offering similar work to the child. Judgements can be made about whether the child is being offered too many or too few people and programmes. Similarly, whether parents are being asked to do too many things at home. Parents, typically, are concerned when their infant's practitioners do not talk to each other, leaving the parent as the go-between. This is disrespectful to the infant and family and puts yet one more demand on the parent.

Stage 2:

Practitioners and parents adopt relevant parts of each other's approaches. This can increase the infant's opportunities for learning and practising particular tasks and facilitate the interplay between their various activities and abilities. For instance, each can offer the infant practice in the agreed signs, symbols or spoken words, each can incorporate the same postures and movements into their work with the child when it is appropriate.

Stage 3:

Practitioners and parents can work towards some degree of actually joining together the infant's development and learning programmes. This can be helped by agreeing to move from planning a discipline-based 'physiotherapy programme' or 'speech and language therapy programme' to a child-based 'getting dressed programme', a 'mealtime programme' or 'a playing on the floor and moving around the room programme'. In this way the infant gets whole-child learning opportunities in relevant situations and times and with natural opportunities to join abilities together. One outcome of this sharing process is 'collective competence'.

Stage 4:

It might be decided that one person could take on the work of another using the 'consultant model' in which one person hands over some part of their work with an infant to another TAC member who is competent to take it on with necessary support. This will reduce the number of people doing regular hands-on work with the child. This has direct advantage to the child, reduces the number of necessary sessions at home or in clinics, and supports service providers in their efforts to make the best use of their limited resources.

Stage 5:

The consultant model described above can progress, by TAC decision, into agreeing one of the team as the single primary interventionist who becomes for an agreed period of time the one practitioner doing most of the regular hands-on work with the child. The working unit now becomes a team of three (or four) – infant, parent (or parents) and primary interventionist.

*

[The text in this appendix is extracted from *Early Childhood Intervention without Tears*, pp 35-36.]

References

Bartram, P. (2009) The Eye of the Sea - A response to the article, TAC for the 21st century: A unifying theory about children who have multifaceted disabilities. *Interconnections Quarterly Journal,* **7**, p 6

Boucher, S et al. (2018) *'Are you worried about your child?' A guide to support families of children with complex needs and the professionals who care for them.* http://www.tacinterconnections.com/images/Guide2-to-Support-Families-of-Children-with-Complex-Needs.pdf

Davis, H. (2010) The Helping Relationship: Understanding Partnerships. *Interconnections Quarterly Journal,* **6,** p 23

Davis, H. & Day, C. (2010) *Working in Partnership: The Family Partnership Model.* London: Pearson

Hanh, T. N. (1987) *Interbeing: Commentaries on the Tiep Hien Precepts.* Berkeley: Parallax Press

Levitt, S. (1994) *Basic Abilities: A whole approach.* UK: Souvenir Press

Limbrick, P. (2001) *Team Around the Child: Multi-agency service co-ordination for children with complex needs and their families.* UK: Interconnections

Limbrick, P. (2003) *An Integrated Pathway for Assessment and Support: For children with complex needs and their families,* UK: Interconnections

Limbrick, P. (2004) *Early Support for Children with Complex Needs: Team Around the Child and the multi-agency keyworker.* Worcester; Interconnections

Limbrick, P. ed. (2007) *Family-centred support for children with disabilities and special need: A collection of essays.* Clifford: Interconnections

Limbrick, P. (2009) *TAC for the 21st Century: Nine essays on Team Around the Child.* UK: Interconnections

Limbrick, P. (2012) *Horizontal Teamwork in a Vertical World: Exploring interagency collaboration and people empowerment.* Clifford: Interconnections

Limbrick, P. (2016) *Caring Activism: A 21st century concept of care.* Clifford: Interconnections

Limbrick, P. (2017) *Early Childhood Intervention without Tears: Improved support for infants with disabilities and their families.* Clifford: Interconnections

Limbrick, P. (2018) *Primary Interventionists in the TAC Approach: A guide for managers and practitioners supporting families whose baby or infant has a multifaceted condition.* Clifford: Interconnections

Limbrick, P. (2019) *Zen in care and support for new children who have disabilities.* http://www.tacinterconnections.com/index.php/allnews/developmentsintreatment/3085-zen-in-care-and-support-for-new-children-who-have-disabilities

Limbrick-Spencer, G. (2001) *The Keyworker: a practical guide.* Birmingham: WordWorks with Handsel Trust

Polatajko, H. J., Townsend, E. A. & Craik, J. (2007). The Canadian Model of Occupational Performance and Engagement (CMOP-E). In E. A. Townsend & H. J. Polatajko (eds.), *Enabling Occupation II: Advancing an Occupational Therapy Vision of Health, Well-being, & Justice through Occupation*, Ottawa, ON: CAOT Publications ACE. 22-36.

Werner, D. (1987) *Disabled Village Children: A guide for community health workers, rehabilitation workers, and families.* Berkeley: Hesperian

Family Fund website: https://www.familyfund.org.uk/

NICE website: https://www.nice.org.uk/

OFSTED website: https://www.gov.uk/government/organisations/ofsted

[To access Interconnections documents, please contact peter.limbrick@teamaroundthechild.com]